Interior Environment, and Related Agencies Appropriations

INTERIOR ENVIRONMENT, AND RELATED AGENCIES APPROPRIATIONS

CAROL HARDY VINCENT,
ROBERT BAMBERGER,
DAVID M. BEARDEN
AND
M. LYNNE CORN

Nova Science Publishers, Inc.
New York

For permission to use material from this book please contact us:
Telephone 631-231-7269; Fax 631-231-8175
Web Site: http://www.novapublishers.com

LIBRARY OF CONGRESS CATALOGING-IN-PUBLICATION DATA

Interior, Environment,nd related agencies appropriations.Carol Hardy Vincent…[et al].

p. cm.

ISBN 978-1-60456-665-9(softcover)

1.United States. Dept. of the Interior—Appropriations and expenditures.2.United States. Environmental Protection Agency—Appropriations and expenditures.3. United Stated—Appropriations and expenditures.I. Vincent,Carol Hardy.

KF5605.I58 2008

343.73'034—dc22 2008018969

Published by Nova Science Publishers, Inc. ✢ New York

CONTENTS

Preface		**vii**
Chapter 1	Most Recent Developments	**1**
Chapter 2	Introduction	**3**
Chapter 3	FY2008 Budget and Appropriations	**7**
Chapter 4	Title I: Department of the Interior	**15**
Chapter 5	Title II: Environmental Protection Agency	**63**
Chapter 6	Title III: Related Agencies	**75**
Chapter 7	Cross-Cutting Topics	**97**
References		**113**
Index		**119**

PREFACE*

The annual consideration of appropriations bills (regular, continuing, and supplemental) by Congress is part of a complex set of budget processes that also encompasses the consideration of budget resolutions, revenue and debt-limit legislation, other spending measures, and reconciliation bills. In addition, the operation of programs and the spending of appropriated funds are subject to constraints established in authorizing statutes. Congressional action on the budget for a fiscal year usually begins following the submission of the President's budget at the beginning of the session. Congressional practices governing the consideration of appropriations and other budgetary measures are rooted in the Constitution, the standing rules of the House and Senate, and statutes, such as the Congressional Budget and Impoundment Control Act of 1974.

This book is a guide to one of the regular appropriations bills that Congress considers each year. It is designed to supplement the information provided by the House and Senate Subcommittees on Interior, Environment, and Related Agencies. It summarizes the status of the Interior, Environment, and Related Agencies appropriations bill, its scope, major issues, funding levels, and related congressional activity.

The Interior, Environment, and Related Agencies appropriations bill includes funding for the Department of the Interior (DOI), except for the Bureau of Reclamation, and for two agencies within other departments — the Forest Service within the Department of Agriculture and the Indian Health Service (IHS) within the Department of Health and Human Services.

* Excerpted from CRS Report RL340114, dated February 3, 2008.

It also includes funding for arts and cultural agencies, the Environmental Protection Agency, and numerous other entities.

The Consolidated Appropriations Act for FY2008 (P.L. 110-161) included $26.89 billion for Interior, Environment, and Related Agencies for FY2008. An additional $500.0 million in emergency appropriations for wildfires was included in P.L. 110-116, for an FY2008 total of $27.39 billion. This would be about the same as enacted for FY2007 (including funds for Secure Rural Schools), $240.2 million (0.9%) lower than passed by the House for FY2008 in H.R. 2643, and $205.0 million (0.8%) higher than recommended by the Senate Committee on Appropriations for FY2008 in S. 1696. The FY2008 level was an increase of $1.70 billion (6.6%) over the Administration's request for FY2008.

The FY2008 appropriations level was higher for some agencies than the FY2007 level, but lower for others. Among the FY2008 increases over FY2007 were the following:

- $292.6 million (6.2%) for the Forest Service (FS);
- $185.2 million (9.9%) for the Bureau of Land Management (BLM);
- $166.0 million (5.2%) for the Indian Health Service (IHS);
- $90.4 million (3.9%) for the National Park Service (NPS);
- $47.7 million (7.5%) for the Smithsonian Institution (SI); and
- $28.1 million (2.1%) for the Fish and Wildlife Service (FWS).

Among the FY2008 decreases from FY2007 were the following:

- $263.6 million (3.4%) for the Environmental Protection Agency (EPA);
- $124.2 million (42.2%) for the Office of Surface Mining Reclamation and Enforcement (OSM);
- $43.6 million (27.3%) for the Minerals Management Service (MMS); and
- $33.9 million (15.2%) for the Office of Special Trustee for American Indians (OST).

Congress debated a variety of funding and policy issues during consideration of FY2008 Interior appropriations legislation. They included appropriate funding for BIA construction, education, and housing; IHS construction and urban Indian health; wastewater/drinking water needs; land acquisition; the Payments in Lieu of Taxes program; the Superfund program; the Smithsonian Institution; and wildland fire fighting. Other issues included

Indian trust fund management, leasing in the Outer Continental Shelf, and royalty relief.

Chapter 1

MOST RECENT DEVELOPMENTS

The Consolidated Appropriations Act for FY2008 (P.L. 110-161) provided $26.89 billion for Interior, Environment, and Related Agencies. Another $500.0 million in emergency funds for wildfires was provided in P.L. 110-116, for an FY2008 total of $27.39 billion.

Chapter 2

INTRODUCTION

The annual Interior, Environment, and Related Agencies appropriations bill includes funding for agencies and programs in three separate federal departments, as well as numerous related agencies and bureaus. It provides funding for Department of the Interior (DOI) agencies (except for the Bureau of Reclamation, funded in Energy and Water Development appropriations laws), many of which manage land and other natural resource or regulatory programs. The bill also provides funds for agencies in two other departments — the Forest Service in the Department of Agriculture, and the Indian Health Service (IHS) in the Department of Health and Human Services — as well as funds for the Environmental Protection Agency (EPA). Further, the annual bill includes funding for arts and cultural agencies, such as the Smithsonian Institution, National Gallery of Art, National Endowment for the Arts, and National Endowment for the Humanities, and for numerous other entities and agencies.

In recent years, the appropriations laws for Interior and Related Agencies provided funds for several activities within the Department of Energy (DOE), including research, development, and conservation programs; the Naval Petroleum Reserves; and the Strategic Petroleum Reserve. However, at the outset of the 109th Congress, these DOE programs were transferred to the House and Senate Appropriations subcommittees covering energy and water, to consolidate jurisdiction over DOE.[1] At the same time, jurisdiction over the EPA and several smaller entities was moved to the House and Senate Appropriations subcommittees covering Interior and Related Agencies.[2] This change resulted from the abolition of the House and Senate Appropriations Subcommittees on Veterans Affairs, Housing and

Urban Development, and Independent Agencies, which previously had jurisdiction over EPA.

Since FY2006, appropriations laws for Interior, Environment, and Related Agencies have contained three primary titles providing funding. This book is organized along these lines. Accordingly, the first section (Title I) provides information on Interior agencies; the second section (Title II) discusses EPA; and the third section (Title III) addresses other agencies, programs, and entities. A fourth section of this book discusses cross-cutting topics that encompass more than one agency.

Entries in this book are for major agencies (e.g., the National Park Service) and cross-cutting issues (e.g., Everglades restoration) that receive funding in the Interior, Environment, and Related Agencies appropriations bill. For each such agency or issue, we discuss some of the key funding changes proposed or enacted for FY2008 that are likely to be of interest to Congress. We also address related policy issues that occurred in the context of considering appropriations legislation. Presenting such information in summary form is a challenge given that budget submissions for some agencies number several hundred pages and contain innumerable funding, programmatic, and legislative changes for congressional consideration. Similarly, funding bills and accompanying reports contain numerous line items and discussions of programs and issues.

This book contains final FY2007 enacted levels for agencies, programs, and activities. The Administration did not use these figures as the basis of comparison in agency budget submissions for FY2008, because agencies were being funded under a short-term continuing resolution at the time of those submissions. Accordingly, the FY2007 figures used throughout this book will differ in many cases from those contained in the FY2008 agency budget submissions. A further difference is that FY2007 figures in this book include supplemental funding.[3]

Final FY2007 funding levels, as contained in this book, were determined by the agencies under the provisions of P.L. 110-5, the Revised Continuing Appropriations Resolution for FY2007. Continuing funding was needed to fund agency operations and activities because Congress did not enact a regular FY2007 appropriations bill for Interior, Environment, and Related Agencies. P.L. 110-5 provided funds though September 30, 2007, which was the rest of the fiscal year. It continued funds at the FY2006 account level, except where otherwise specified. The law required that agencies and departments submit an allocation of funds below the account level, for example for programs and activities, to the House and Senate

Appropriations Committees. The submissions were due within 30 days of enactment (March 17, 2007).

In general, in this book the term *appropriations* represents total funds available, including regular annual and supplemental appropriations, as well as rescissions, transfers, and deferrals, but excludes permanent mandatory budget authorities. Increases and decreases generally are calculated on comparisons between the funding levels enacted for FY2008 and those enacted for FY2007 and requested by the President for FY2008. The House Committee on Appropriations is the primary source of the funding figures used throughout the book. Other sources of information include the Senate Committee on Appropriations, agency budget justifications, and the *Congressional Record.* In the tables throughout this book, some columns of funding figures do not add to the precise totals provided due to rounding.

FY2004-FY2008

Table 1, below, shows the budget authority for Interior, Environment, and Related Agencies for FY2004-FY2008. Funding for earlier years is not readily available due to the changes in the makeup of the Interior appropriations bill. The President's request for FY2008 ($25.69 billion), if enacted, would have been the lowest level since FY2004. It would have been a $1.64 billion (6%) decrease in funds from the FY2004 level in current dollars, or a 16% decrease in constant dollars (assuming 2.24% inflation for 2007 and 2008). The House-approved funding of $27.63 billion was slightly higher than FY2004 — a $301.8 million increase (1%) in current dollars but a 10% decrease in constant dollars. The Senate Committee on Appropriations recommended $27.19 billion, which was a slightly lower level than FY2004 — a $143.3 million decrease (0.5%) in current dollars and an 11% decrease in constant dollars. For FY2008, the $26.89 billion contained in the Consolidated Appropriations Act was a decrease of $483.3 million (2%) in current dollars and a 12% decrease in constant dollars. The FY2008 total funding of $27.39 billion, including the $500.0 million in emergency fire funding, would be a $61.7 million increase (0.2%) over FY2004 in current dollars but a 10% decrease in constant dollars. See table 24 for a budgetary history of each agency for FY2004-FY2008.

Table 1. Interior, Environment, and Related Agencies Appropriations, FY2004 to FY2008 (budget authority in billions of current dollars)

FY2004	FY2005	FY2006	FY2007	FY2008
$27.33	$27.02	$25.94	$27.38	$27.39

Note: These figures exclude permanent budget authorities, and generally do not reflect scorekeeping adjustments. They generally reflect rescissions and supplemental appropriations to date, except that the FY2006 figure does not reflect supplementals. The FY2007 figure includes $425.0 million for Secure Rural Schools.

Chapter 3

FY2008 BUDGET AND APPROPRIATIONS

CURRENT OVERVIEW

FY2008 funding for Interior, Environment, and Related Agencies was included in the Consolidated Appropriations Act for FY2008 (P.L. 110-161). The enacted bill (H.R. 2764), providing funding for government agencies and activities except defense, was signed into law on December 26, 2007. An explanatory statement on the bill was printed in the *Congressional Record* of December 17, 2007. The explanatory statement on Interior, Environment, and Related Agencies (Division F of the bill) was published in Book II of the *Record*, at H16122-H16178. The explanatory statement noted that it contained "a list of congressional earmarks and congressionally directed spending items" as defined in House and Senate rules, at H16142-H16157. However, the amounts in the list did not reflect a 1.56% across-the-board cut provided in H.R. 2764 for Interior, Environment, and Related Agencies. The explanatory statement also included a detailed funding table for Interior, at H16158-H16178. For activities, programs, and agencies, the table contained funding levels enacted for FY2007, requested by the Administration for FY2008, approved by the House for FY2008, recommended by the Senate Committee on Appropriations for FY2008, contained in H.R. 2764 for FY2008, and reduced by a 1.56% across-the-board cut for FY2008.

The Consolidated Appropriations Act for FY2008 (P.L. 110-161) provided $26.89 billion for Interior, Environment, and Related Agencies for FY2008. That total reflects the 1.56% cut provided in the Interior portion of the act. In general, FY2008 appropriations figures used throughout this book also reflect the cut, which under the law was to be applied across the board to programs, projects, and activities. An additional $500.0 million in emergency appropriations for FY2008 for wildfires was included in an earlier law, P.L. 110-116, for an FY2008 total of $27.39 billion for Interior, Environment, and Related Agencies. This would be about the same as enacted for FY2007 (including funds for Secure Rural Schools), $240.2 million (0.9%) lower than passed by the House for FY2008 in H.R. 2643, and $205.0 million (0.8%) higher than recommended by the Senate Committee on Appropriations for FY2008 in S. 1696. The FY2008 level was an increase of $1.70 billion (6.6%) over the Administration's request.

Of the $500.0 million in P.L. 110-116, $329.0 million was provided to the Forest Service for wildland fire management. The funds were divided as follows: $110.0 million for suppression, $100.0 million for repayment of accounts from which funds were borrowed in FY2007, $80.0 million for hazardous fuels reduction, $25.0 million for rehabilitation and restoration of federal lands, and $14.0 million for construction and reconstruction of federal facilities. For fire fighting on DOI lands, the law provided BLM with the remaining $171.0 million in wildland fire management funds. The funds were apportioned as follows: $40.0 million for suppression, $115.0 million for repayment of accounts from which funds were borrowed in FY2007, $10.0 million for hazardous fuels reduction, and $6.0 million for rehabilitation and restoration of federal lands.

The FY2008 appropriations level was higher for some agencies than the FY2007 level, but lower for others. Among the FY2008 increases over FY2007 were the following:

- $292.6 million (6.2%) for the Forest Service (FS);
- $185.2 million (9.7%) for the Bureau of Land Management (BLM);
- $166.0 million (5.2%) for the Indian Health Service (IHS);
- $90.4 million (3.9%) for the National Park Service (NPS);
- $47.7 million (7.5%) for the Smithsonian Institution (SI); and
- $28.1 million (2.1%) for the Fish and Wildlife Service (FWS).

Among the FY2008 decreases from FY2007 were the following:

- $263.6 million (3.4%) for the Environmental Protection Agency (EPA);
- $124.2 million (42.2%) for the Office of Surface Mining Reclamation and Enforcement (OSM);
- $43.6 million (27.3%) for the Minerals Management Service (MMS); and

- $33.9 million (15.2%) for the Office of Special Trustee for American Indians (OST).

Prior to the enactment of the consolidated bill, Interior, Environment, and Related Agencies were funded under a series of laws that generally continued funds at FY2007 levels. Continuing funding was needed to fund ongoing projects and activities because Congress did not enact a regular FY2008 funding bill for Interior, Environment, and Related Agencies before the October 1, 2007, start of the fiscal year.

In earlier action, the Senate Committee on Appropriations had reported a regular annual appropriations bill, but it was not considered on the Senate floor. Specifically, on June 26, 2007, the Senate committee reported S. 1696 (S.Rept. 110-91), with $27.19 billion for FY2008 for all agencies included in the Interior, Environment, and Related Agencies appropriations bill. On June 27, 2007, the House passed H.R. 2643 with $27.63 billion for FY2008. The House-passed level would have been an increase over the FY2007 level of $27.38 billion, including $425.0 million for the Secure Rural Schools program (established under P.L. 106-393). The Senate committee level would have been a decrease from FY2007. The House and the Senate committee levels both would have been increases over the President's request for FY2008 of $25.69 billion.

The Senate Appropriations Committee considered several amendments during its markup, in addition to a managers' package of amendments. The Committee agreed to an amendment to remove language from the bill that barred funds from being used for new Outer Continental Shelf leases for those holding leases without price thresholds, unless the leases were renegotiated. The Committee also agreed to an amendment seeking to ban imports of polar bears and polar bear parts. An amendment seeking to extend the Secure Rural Schools Act for four years was withdrawn. The act provides a method for compensating counties for the tax exempt status of most national forests (managed by the FS) and some public lands (managed by the BLM). Amendments seeking to expedite the time frame for filing claims challenging the land management plan for the Tongass National Forest (AK) also were withdrawn.

The House considered 58 amendments to H.R. 2643 during two days of floor debate, and adopted 18 of them before passing the bill (272-155) on June 27, 2007. The amendments addressed an array of programs and issues. Some of them were broad, as in those that sought to cut the total appropriation in the bill by a particular sum or reduce each appropriation in the bill by a fixed percentage (which were not agreed to). Others were more narrow, such as those prohibiting funds in the bill from being used for particular programs or purposes. Many of the amendments are discussed in the pertinent sections throughout this book.

In earlier action, on June 11, 2007, the House Appropriations Committee had reported H.R. 2643 (H.Rept. 110-187) with a total of $27.63 billion. The House Appropriations Committee issued a supplemental report (H.Rept. 110-187, Part II) on June 22, 2007. The report identified projects that would be funded from various line items in the bill, such as the construction accounts of the land management agencies. It specified whether the Administration or a particular Member of Congress requested the funding and the state in which the project is located.

MAJOR ISSUES

Controversial funding and policy issues typically have been debated during consideration of the annual Interior, Environment, and Related Agencies Appropriations bill. Debate on the FY2008 funding levels encompassed a variety of issues, many of which have been controversial in the past, including the issues listed below.

- *Clean Water and Drinking Water State Revolving Funds*, especially the adequacy of funding to meet state and local wastewater and drinking water needs. These state revolving funds provide seed money for state loans to communities for wastewater and drinking water infrastructure projects. (For more information, see the "Environmental Protection Agency" section in this book.)
- *Construction of BIA Schools and IHS Health Facilities*, particularly whether to enact funding cuts proposed in the President's FY2008 budget. (For more information, see the "Bureau of Indian Affairs" and the "Indian Health Service" sections in this book.)
- *Indian Trust Funds*, especially whether to enact reductions proposed in the President's FY2008 request and the method by which a historical accounting will be conducted of Individual Indian Money (IIM) accounts to determine correct balances in the class-action lawsuit against the government. (For more information, see the "Office of Special Trustee for American Indians" section in this book.)
- *Land Acquisition*, including the appropriate level of funding for the Land and Water Conservation Fund for federal land acquisition and

the state grant program, and extent to which the fund should be used for activities not involving land acquisition. (For more information, see "The Land and Water Conservation Fund (LWCF)" section in this book.)

- *Outer Continental Shelf Leasing*, particularly the moratoria on preleasing and leasing activities in offshore areas, and oil and gas leases in offshore California. (For more information, see the "Minerals Management Service" section in this book.)
- *Payments in Lieu of Taxes Program (PILT)*, primarily the appropriate level of funding for compensating local governments for federal land within their jurisdictions. (For more information, see the "Payments in Lieu of Taxes Program (PILT)" section in this book.)
- *Royalty Relief,* especially the extent to which oil and natural gas companies receive royalty relief for production of oil and natural gas on federal lands. (For more information see "MMS" section of this book.)
- *Superfund*, notably the adequacy of proposed funding to meet hazardous waste cleanup needs, and whether to continue using general Treasury revenues to fund the account or reinstate a tax on industry that originally paid for most of the program. (For more information, see the "Environmental Protection Agency" section in this book.)
- *Termination of BIA Education and Housing and IHS Urban Health Programs*, particularly whether to end funding for BIA's Johnson-O'Malley grants to schools and the Housing Improvement Program and for IHS's urban Indian health projects. (For more information, see the "Bureau of Indian Affairs" and the "Indian Health Service" sections in this book.)
- *Wildland Fire Fighting*, involving questions about the appropriate level of funding to fight fires on agency lands; advisability of borrowing funds from other agency programs to fight wildfires; implementation of a new program for wildland fire protection and locations for fire protection treatments; and impact of environmental analysis, public involvement, and challenges to agency decisions on fuel reduction activities. (For more information, see the "Bureau of Land Management" and "Forest Service" sections in this book.)

Table 2. Status of Interior, Environment, and Related Agencies Appropriations, FY2008

Subcommittee Markup		House Report	House Passage	Senate Report	Senate Passage	Conf. Report	Conference Report Approval		Public Law
House	Senate						House	Senate	
05/23/07	06/19/07	H.R. 2643 H.Rept. 110-187 06/11/07; Part II 06/22/07	H.R. 2643 06/27/07 272-155	S. 1696 S.Rept. 110-91 06/26/07	—	—	—	—	H.R. 2764 P.L. 110-161 12/26/07

STATUS OF BILL

Table 2 contains information on congressional consideration of the FY2008 Interior appropriations bill.

Chapter 4

TITLE I: DEPARTMENT OF THE INTERIOR

BUREAU OF LAND MANAGEMENT

Overview

The Bureau of Land Management (BLM) manages approximately 258 million acres of public land for diverse and sometimes conflicting uses, such as energy and minerals development, livestock grazing, recreation, and preservation. The agency also is responsible for about 700 million acres of federal subsurface mineral resources throughout the nation, and supervises the mineral operations on an estimated 56 million acres of Indian Trust lands. Another key BLM function is wildland fire management on about 370 million acres of DOI, other federal, and certain nonfederal land.

For the BLM, the FY2008 law contained $1.89 billion, including $78.0 million in emergency appropriations for wildfire suppression contained in Title V. An additional $171.0 million in emergency wildfire funds was provided in an earlier law, P.L. 110-116, for a total BLM appropriation of $2.06 billion for FY2008. This level was higher than enacted for FY2007 and had been supported for FY2008 by the Administration, House, and Senate Appropriations Committee, primarily due to the emergency appropriations for wildfires. See table 3. Proposed funding for several key activities is discussed below.

Table 3. Appropriations for the Bureau of Land Management, FY2007-FY2008 ($ in millions)

Bureau of Land Management	FY2007 Approp.	FY2008 Request	FY2008 House Passed	FY2008 Senate Comm.	FY2008 Approp.
Management of Lands and Resources	866.9	879.4	888.6	902.9	853.9
Wildland Fire Management[a]	853.4	801.8	806.6	829.5	1,057.1
— *Preparedness*	*274.9*	*268.3*	*274.9*	*286.0*	*276.5*
— *Suppression*[a]	*344.2*	*294.4*	*294.4*	*294.4*	*367.8*
— *Other Operations*	*234.3*	*239.1*	*237.4*	*249.1*	*241.8*
— *Emergency Appropriations (P.L. 110-116)*	—	—	—	—	*171.0*
Construction	11.8	6.5	6.5	11.5	6.4
Land Acquisition	8.6	1.6	18.6	12.2	8.9
Oregon and California Grant Lands	109.0	110.2	110.2	110.2	108.5
Range Improvements	10.0	10.0	10.0	10.0	10.0
Service Charges, Deposits, and Forfeitures[b]	0.0	0.0	0.0	0.0	0.0
Miscellaneous Trust Funds	12.4	12.4	12.4	12.4	12.4
Total Appropriations[a]	1,872.0	1,822.0	1,853.0	1,888.7	2,057.2

[a]. The figures for FY2007 reflect a supplemental appropriation of $95.0 million for wildfire suppression contained in P.L. 110-28. The figures for FY2008 appropriated reflect an emergency appropriation of $78.0 million for suppression included in Title V of the FY2008 law. The FY2008 appropriation figures for wildland fire management and BLM total also include $171.0 million in emergency appropriations provided in P.L. 110-116.

[b]. The figures of "0" are a result of an appropriation matched by offsetting fees.

Management of Lands and Resources

Management of Lands and Resources includes funds for an array of BLM land programs, including protection, recreational use, improvement, development, disposal, and general BLM administration. For this line item, the FY2008 law contained $853.9 million, lower than enacted for FY2007 and supported by the President, House, and Senate Appropriations Committee for FY2008. The enacted level reflects $25.5 million in revenues from a new oil and gas cost recovery program as an offset to the appropriation for energy and minerals management. Many lands and resources programs received increases relative to FY2007, while others received decreased or level funding.

For maintenance, the FY2008 law included $74.8 million, a $4.4 million increase over the FY2007 level. Increases were included for both annual and deferred maintenance, with total deferred maintenance funding of $36.5 million. BLM has estimated its deferred maintenance at between $387 million and $473 million for FY2006. Wildlife and fisheries would receive $44.3 million in FY2008, a $3.5 million increase. For range management, the law contained $73.0 million, $4.8 million more than appropriated for FY2007. More than half the increase for each of wildlife and fisheries and for range management was for the healthy lands initiative (see below). Recreation and wilderness programs received $67.9 million, up $4.2 million.

For the healthy lands initiative, the FY2008 law provided about $5 million, an increase above the $3.0 million appropriated for FY2007. The initiative consists of vegetation resources enhancements to restore and improve the health and productivity of western public lands. The House, like the Administration, had sought a large increase — to $15.0 million — while the Senate Committee had recommended $6.0 million. The Administration had anticipated using another $8.2 million in existing BLM funds, and leveraging $10.0 million in contributions from partners. For the National Landscape Conservation System (NLCS), which consists of 26 million acres of BLM's protected conservation areas, the FY2008 law provided about $5 million over the President's request of $49.2 million. The House and the Senate Appropriations Committee had approved higher increases over the request. In the explanatory statement, the appropriations committees directed BLM to present annual NLCS reports with expenditures by unit and subactivity to enhance fiscal accountability.

The FY2008 law included lower funding for energy and minerals, $109.9 million, than had been enacted for FY2007 — $138.1 million (including Alaska minerals). The reduction is to be accomplished primarily through the collection of $25.5 million in offsetting fees. These revenues are expected to be derived through a new program requiring payment of $4,000 for each application for a permit to drill oil and gas wells. A similar program had been requested by the Administration and supported by the House. The FY2008 law capped the appropriation for oil and gas management at $90.2 million, due to concerns that BLM has used conservation and other natural resource funds for oil and gas activities (H.Rept. 110-187, p. 16). Further, the law prohibited funds from being used to prepare final regulations regarding a commercial leasing program for oil shale or to conduct a commercial oil shale lease sale. In the explanatory statement, the appropriations committees expressed that while oil shale has the potential to be an important energy resource, there is concern that DOI "may be moving ahead before the full impacts of such a program are known, and without full and complete cooperation of the affected States ... Colorado, Utah, and Wyoming."[4] Current law (P.L. 109-58) requires BLM to issue the regulations and to move to a commercial leasing program.

For management of wild horses and burros, the FY2008 law provided nearly level funding — $36.2 million. The Administration had sought to reduce funding to $32.1 million, but the House and the Senate Committee supported increases over FY2007. In its report, the Senate Appropriations Committee "strongly" encouraged federal agencies that use horses to first seek to acquire a wild horse from BLM, and encouraged BLM to expedite providing wild horses to state and local police (S.Rept. 110-91, p. 12).

Wildland Fire Management

For Wildland Fire Management, the FY2008 law contained $886.1 million, including the $78.0 million in emergency appropriations for wildfire suppression. This was an increase over the FY2007 level and the levels supported by the President, House, and Senate Committee for FY2008. An additional $171.0 million was provided in P.L. 110-116, for suppression, hazardous fuels reduction, rehabilitation, and repayment of accounts from which funds were borrowed in FY2007 for fire suppression. With these funds, the FY2008 total for wildland fire management was $1.06 billion, which is about half the overall BLM appropriation for FY2008.

Fire suppression would increase from $344.2 million in FY2007 (including supplemental funding) to $367.8 million in FY2008 under P.L. 110-161. This would fund the ten-year average cost of fire suppression (about $289.8 million) and provide additional funds ($78.0 million) if needed for an extreme fire season, according to the explanatory statement on the FY2008 bill. Preparedness was increased from $274.9 million in FY2007 to $276.5 million in FY2008. The Administration had sought to reduce preparedness funding, while the House had supported level funding. The Senate Committee had recommended an increase on the grounds that cutting preparedness funding does not save money, but shifts expenditures to suppression (S.Rept. 110-91, p. 15). Funding for other fire operations would increase from $234.3 million in FY2007 to $241.8 million in FY2008, primarily due to the inclusion of $5.9 million for rural fire assistance. Most of the funding for other operations in FY2008 was for hazardous fuels reduction — $199.6 million —essentially level with FY2007 funding. In the explanatory statement, appropriators directed the agencies to report on the allocation of funds for reducing hazardous fuels.

The wildland fire funds appropriated to BLM are used for fire fighting on all DOI lands. Interior appropriations laws also provide funds for wildland fire management to the Forest Service (Department of Agriculture) for fire programs primarily on its lands. A focus of both departments is implementing the Healthy Forests Restoration Act of 2003 (P.L. 108-148) and the National Fire Plan, which emphasize reducing hazardous fuels which can contribute to catastrophic fires. (For additional information, see the "Forest Service" section in this book.)

Construction

For FY2008, the law contained $6.4 million for BLM Construction, akin to the level requested by the Administration and supported by the House. The explanatory statement expressed that the funds should be allocated as described in the President's budget request, which called for 12 construction projects in five states. The FY2008 level was a decrease of $5.4 million from FY2007 ($11.8 million). The Senate Appropriations Committee had supported funding at nearly the FY2007 level, to avoid an increase in the construction backlog, and had expressed "disapproval" regarding DOI's "lack of commitment to its infrastructure" (S.Rept. 110-91, p. 15-16).

Land Acquisition

For Land Acquisition for FY2008, the law contained $8.9 million, a small increase over the FY2007 level of $8.6 million. The explanatory statement specified how about two-thirds of the funds would be used for eight acquisitions. Both the House and the Senate Committee initially had supported higher increases for FY2008. However, the Administration had sought a reduction to $1.6 million, with an additional $5.0 million from the proceeds of sales of the subsurface mineral estate to the surface owners. BLM estimated that 500,000 acres could be sold annually for approximately $10 per acre, for a total of $5.0 million per year. Such a redirection of the proceeds of the sales to land acquisition was not included in the FY2008 law. The appropriation for BLM acquisitions had fallen steadily from $49.9 million in FY2002 to $8.6 million for FY2007. Money for land acquisition is appropriated from the Land and Water Conservation Fund. (For more information, see the "Land and Water Conservation Fund (LWCF)" section in this book.)

For further information on the *Bureau of Land Management*, see its website at [http://www.blm.gov/nhp/index.htm].

CRS Report RL33792. Federal Lands Managed by the Bureau of Land Management (BLM) and the Forest Service: Issues for the 110th Congress, by Ross W. Gorte, Carol Hardy Vincent, and Marc Humphries.

CRS Report RL33990. *Wildfire Funding*, by Ross W. Gorte.

Fish and Wildlife Service

For FY2008, the appropriation for the Fish and Wildlife Service (FWS) was $1.37 billion. The FY2008 level was a 2% increase over the FY2007 level of $1.34 billion and a 6% increase over the President's request of $1.29 billion. The House had approved $1.42 billion, while the Senate Appropriations Committee had recommended $1.38 billion.

By far the largest portion of the FWS annual appropriation is for the Resource Management account. The FY2008 appropriation for this account was $1.08 billion, a 6% increase over the FY2007 level of $1.02 billion and a 5% increase over the Administration's request of $1.03 billion. The House had approved $1.10 billion; the Senate Committee level was $1.08 billion.

Among the programs included in Resources Management are the Endangered Species program, the Refuge System, and Law Enforcement.

Endangered Species Funding

Funding for the Endangered Species program is one of the perennially controversial portions of the FWS budget. The FY2008 appropriation was $150.5 million for the Endangered Species program, a 4% increase over FY2007. The Administration had proposed a smaller increase of 1% — from $144.7 million in FY2007 to $146.5 million in FY2008. See table 4. The FY2008 law did not include language from the Senate committee bill that had sought to limit funding for the importation of polar bear parts taken in sport hunts. The House had rejected a similar amendment during floor debate. The House had also rejected an amendment to prohibit use of funds for Mexican wolf recovery.

A number of related programs also benefit conservation of species that are listed, or proposed for listing, under the Endangered Species Act. The President proposed to end the Landowner Incentive Program ($23.7 million in FY2007) as well as Stewardship Grants ($7.3 million in FY2007). The President also sought to reduce the Cooperative Endangered Species Conservation Fund (for grants to states and territories to conserve threatened and endangered species) from $81.0 million to $80.0 million. The FY2008 appropriation reflected these proposals, and included a further reduction for the Cooperative Endangered Species program for an FY2008 appropriation of $73.8 million. However, the FY2008 law also provided for the use of $5.0 million in prior year balances, making total FY2008 funding of $78.8 million for the Cooperative Endangered Species program. See table 4.

In total, the FY2008 appropriations law contained $224.3 million for endangered species and related programs, down 13% from the FY2007 level of $256.6 million. Under the President's request, total FY2008 funding would have decreased to $226.5 million, a 12% reduction.

Table 4. Appropriations for Endangered Species and Related Programs, FY2007-FY2008 (\$ in thousands)

Endangered Species and Related Programs	FY2007 Approp.	FY2008 Request	FY2008 House Passed	FY2008 Senate Comm.	FY2008 Approp.
Endangered Species Program					
— *Candidate Conservation*	*8,425*	*8,635*	*9,135*	*10,135*	*9,731*
— *Listing*	*17,824*	*18,263*	*18,763*	*18,763*	*17,978*
— *Consultation*	*49,179*	*51,578*	*52,578*	*53,578*	*51,758*
— *Recovery*	*69,244*	*68,067*	*72,067*	*73,067*	*71,041*
Subtotal, Endangered Species Program	144,672	146,543	152,543	155,543	150,508
Related Programs					
— *Landowner Incentive Program*	*23,667*	*0*	*0*	*0*	*0*
— *Private Stewardship Grants*	*7,277*	*0*	*0*	*0*	*0*
— *Cooperative Endangered Species Conservation Fund*	*81,001*	*80,001*	*81,001*	*80,001*	*73,754*[a]
Subtotal, Related Programs	111,945	80,001	81,001	80,001	73,754
Total Appropriations	256,617	226,544	233,544	235,544	224,262

[a]. An additional \$5.0 million in prior year funds was provided for FY2008.

National Wildlife Refuge System (NWRS) and Law Enforcement

For refuge operations and maintenance, the FY2008 appropriation was \$434.1 million. This was a 10% increase over the FY2007 level of \$395.3 million. The President had proposed \$394.8 million, a slight decrease from FY2007. However, both the House and the Senate Appropriations Committee had sought increases. The House had approved \$451.0 million, an increase of 14%, while the Senate committee level was \$413.8 million, up 5%.

Costs of operation have increased on many refuges, partly due to special problems such as hurricane damage and more aggressive border enforcement. Reductions in funding for operations in the NWRS, combined with the need to meet fixed costs such as rent, salaries, and utilities, have led to cuts in funding for programs to aid endangered species, reduce infestation by invasive species, protect water supplies, address habitat restoration, and ensure staffing at the less popular refuges. The Northeast Region (roughly Virginia to Maine, with 71 refuges) took the lead in addressing this issue by attempting to consolidate management at refuges, and increasing the number of refuges which are not staffed on a regular basis (termed "de-staffing"). This region also attempted to consolidate some services in order to spread remaining resources more effectively. Other regions have begun their own plans to address reduced operating budgets. In the Explanatory Statement for FY2008, FWS was directed to use the additional FY2008 funding to reestablish basic operations nationwide. FWS was further directed to report back to the Appropriations Committees on allocation of the increased funding within 60 days.

The FY2008 appropriations law contained $59.6 million for Law Enforcement, a 4% increase over the FY2007 level of $57.3 million. The President had proposed $57.6 million, a modest increase over FY2007, but the House and the Senate Appropriations Committee had sought larger increases. Specifically, the House had approved $60.1 million, up 5%, while the Senate committee recommended $61.1 million, a 7% increase.

Avian Flu

For FY2008, Congress enacted $7.3 million for the study, monitoring, and early detection of highly pathogenic avian flu. The Administration, House, and Senate Appropriations Committee initially approved $7.4 million. The FY2007 appropriation was $12.4 million, including a $7.4 million supplemental appropriation in P.L. 110-28. FWS cooperates with other federal and nonfederal agencies in studying the spread of the virus through wild birds. Attention is on North American species whose migratory patterns make them likely to come into contact with infected Asian birds. The geographic focus is on Alaska, the Pacific Flyway (along the west coast), and Pacific islands, with smaller samples in other areas.

Land Acquisition

For FY2008, the appropriation for Land Acquisition was $34.6 million. This was an increase of 92% over the Administration's request and 23% increase over FY2007, with the increase going to the acquisition of new lands and inholdings. The Administration had proposed $18.0 million for

Land Acquisition, $10.0 million (36%) below FY2007. See table 5. In the past, the bulk of this FWS program had been for acquisitions of land for specified federal refuges, but a portion was used for closely related functions such as acquisition management, land exchanges, emergency acquisitions, purchase of inholdings, and general overhead ("Cost Allocation Methodology"). In recent years, less of the funding has been reserved for traditional land acquisition. The Administration had proposed to continue this trend for FY2008, reserving $5.5 million for specified acquisitions, and funding the remainder of the program at $12.5 million.[5] This program is funded with appropriations from LWCF. (For more information, see the "Land and Water Conservation Fund (LWCF)" in this book.)

Table 5. Appropriations for FWS Land Acquisition Program, FY2007-FY2008 ($ in thousands)

FWS Land Acquisition	FY2007 Approp.	FY2008 Request	FY2008 House Passed	FY2008 Senate Comm.	FY2008 Approp.
Acquisitions — Federal Refuge Lands	13,650	5,544	28,650	28,904	20,676
Inholdings	1,500	1,500	1,500	1,500	2,953
Emergencies and Hardships	1,478	1,500	1,478	1,500	0
Exchanges	1,485	1,537	1,485	1,500	1,477
Acquisition Management	8,140	6,436	8,140	8,140	8,013
Cost Allocation Methodology	1,793	1,494	1,793	1,500	1,477
Total Appropriations	28,046	18,011	43,046	43,044	34,596

Wildlife Refuge Fund

The National Wildlife Refuge Fund (also called the Refuge Revenue Sharing Fund) compensates counties for the presence of the nontaxable federal lands of the National Wildlife Refuge System (NWRS). A portion of the fund is supported by the permanent appropriation of receipts from various activities carried out on the NWRS. However, these receipts are not sufficient for full funding of amounts authorized in the formula, and county governments have long urged additional appropriations to make up the difference. Congress generally provides additional appropriations. For FY2008, the appropriation was $14.0 million, a small decrease from the

FY2007 level of $14.2 million. With refuge receipts, the FY2008 level would fund about 42% of the authorized payment level, down from 52% in FY2007. The President had requested $10.8 million for FY2008, down $3.4 million (24%). That level, combined with expected receipts, would have provided about 35% of the authorized full payment. The House had approved the FY2007 level, as did the Senate Appropriations Committee.

Multinational Species and Neotropical Migrants

The Multinational Species Conservation Fund (MSCF) has generated considerable constituent interest despite the small size of the program. It benefits Asian and African elephants, tigers, rhinoceroses, great apes, and marine turtles. For FY2008, the appropriations law contained $7.9 million for MSCF and $4.4 million for the Neotropical Migratory Bird Conservation Fund (NMBCF), both increases over the FY2007 level and the Administration's request for FY2008. The President had proposed $4.3 million for the MSCF and $4.0 million for the NMBCF.[6] The proposal would have cut each of the MSCF programs and held funding level for NMBCF. See table 6.

Table 6. Appropriations for Multinational Species Conservation Fund and Neotropical Migratory Bird Conservation Fund, FY2007-FY2008 ($ in thousands)

Multinational Species Conservation Fund	FY2007 Approp.	FY2008 Request	FY2008 House Passed	FY2008 Senate Comm.	FY2008 Approp.
African Elephant	1,379	990	2,000	1,500	1,477
Tiger and Rhinos	1,576	990	2,500	2,000	1,969
Asian Elephant	1,379	990	2,000	1,500	1,477
Great Apes	1,379	990	2,000	2,000	1,969
Marine Turtles	691	297	1,500	1,000	984
Total MSCF Appropriations	6,404	4,257	10,000	8,000	7,876
Neotropical Migratory Birds	3,941	3,960	5,000	4,000	4,430

State and Tribal Wildlife Grants

State and Tribal Wildlife Grants help fund efforts to conserve species (including nongame species) of concern to states, territories, and tribes. The grants have generated considerable support from these governments. The program was created in the FY2001 Interior appropriations law (P.L. 106-291) and further detailed in subsequent Interior appropriations bills. (It does not have any separate authorizing statute.) Funds may be used to develop state conservation plans as well as to support specific practical conservation projects. A portion of the funding is set aside for competitive grants to tribal governments or tribal wildlife agencies. The remaining portion is for matching grants to states. A state's allocation is determined by formula. The appropriation for FY2008 was $73.8 million. See table 7.

Table 7. Appropriations for State and Tribal Wildlife Grants, FY2007-FY2008 ($ in thousands)

State and Tribal Wildlife Grants	FY2007 Approp.	FY2008 Request	FY2008 House Passed	FY2008 Senate Comm.	FY2008 Approp.
State Grants	61,852	59,210	73,000	60,580	62,724
Competitive Grants for States, Territories, and Other Jurisdictions	0	5,000	5,000	5,000	6,184
Tribal Grants	5,640	5,282	7,000	6,912	4,922
Total Appropriations	67,492	69,492	85,000	72,492	73,830

For further information on the *Fish and Wildlife Service*, see its website at [http://www.fws.gov/].

CRS Report RL33872. *Arctic National Wildlife Refuge (ANWR): New Directions in the 110th Congress*, by M. Lynne Corn, Bernard A. Gelb, and Pamela Baldwin.

CRS Report RL33795. *Avian Influenza in Poultry and Wild Birds*, by Jim Monke and M. Lynne Corn.

CRS Report RL33779. *The Endangered Species Act (ESA) in the 110th Congress: Conflicting Values and Difficult Choices*, by Eugene H. Buck, M. Lynne Corn, Pervaze A. Sheikh, Robert Meltz, and Kristina Alexander.

CRS Report RS21157. *Multinational Species Conservation Fund*, by Pervaze A. Sheikh and M. Lynne Corn.

NATIONAL PARK SERVICE

The National Park Service (NPS) is responsible for the National Park System, currently comprising 391 separate and diverse park units covering 85 million acres. The NPS and its more than 20,000 permanent, temporary, and seasonal employees protect, preserve, interpret, and administer the park system's diverse natural and historic areas representing the cultural identity of the American people. The NPS mission is to protect park resources and values, unimpaired, while making them accessible to the public. Annual park visitation is now 273 million visits. The Park System has some 20 types of area designations, including national parks, monuments, memorials, historic sites, battlefields, seashores, recreational areas, and other classifications. The NPS also supports and promotes some resource conservation activities outside the Park System through limited grant and technical assistance programs and cooperation with partners.

The FY2008 appropriations law provided $2.39 billion for the NPS, $26.6 million (1%) more than the FY2008 request and $90.3 million (4%) above the FY2007 level, but $71.1 million (3%) below the Senate Appropriations Committee level and $122.8 million (5%) below the House total. See table 8. The parks remain popular with the public and the condition of the parks and the adequacy of their care and operating capacity continues to be of concern.

To be ready for the NPS's 100th anniversary in 2016, the Administration proposed a multi-year initiative, beginning in FY2008, to strengthen visitor services and other park programs. The National Parks Centennial Initiative, announced by President Bush in August 2006, could add up to $3 billion in new funds for the parks over the next 10 years through a public/private joint effort. The initiative has three components: (1) a commitment to add $100.0 million annually in discretionary funds; (2) a challenge for the public to donate $100.0 million annually; and (3) a commitment to match the public donations with federal funds of up to $100.0 million annually. The second part of the initiative — the proposed $1 billion "Centennial Challenge" — would rely on corporate, foundation, and other private donations, raising concerns among some park supporters about potential commercialization and privatization influence on the parks. Many claim that the park system has long experienced chronic budget shortfalls. Park advocacy groups have estimated that, on average, the national parks operate with two-thirds of needed funding — a budget shortfall of more than $600 million annually.[7]

Major NPS Issues in Appropriations

The FY2008 law included language proposed by the House extending the authorization of the National Park System Advisory Board until January 1, 2009. Board authority expired on January 1, 2007, preventing statutorily required participation in some NPS programs. The law did not include a transfer of $1.0 million from the Office of the DOI Secretary to park operations to help fully reopen the Statue of Liberty to park visitors, as had been approved by the House.

The Urban Parks and Recreation Recovery (UPARR) grant program has not been funded since FY2002. The House Appropriations Committee reminded the NPS of its responsibility to enforce §1010 of the authorizing legislation (16 U.S.C. §2509), generally prohibiting the conversion of UPARR project sites from public recreational use to other (e.g., commercial) use, regardless of whether funding is provided (H.Rept. 110-187, p. 46). The FY2008 law provided no administrative or new grant monies for UPARR.

The Senate committee bill had directed the NPS to keep in force, for the 2007-2008 winter season, the interim Yellowstone snowmobile use regulations of the past three years. The FY2008 law did not include that language because the NPS issued a Record of Decision (ROD) on winter use management on November 30, 2007, with implementing regulations expected thereafter. Lawsuits challenging the ROD did not request preliminary injunctions, allowing local operations to continue for the 2007-2008 winter season. The Appropriations Committees expressed that this was in the best interest of all parties (Explanatory Statement, H16130-H16131). The FY2008 law retained a provision of the Senate committee bill repealing Section 1077(c) of P.L. 109-364 that had prohibited the NPS from complying with a court-approved agreement to remove nonnative deer and elk from Santa Rosa Island in the Channel Islands National Park. The provision sought to resolve a long-running hunting concession controversy.

Operation of the National Park System

The park operations line item is the primary source of funding for the national parks, accounting for more than 80% of the total NPS budget. The

FY2008 law provided $1.97 billion for park operations, $122.2 million above the FY2007 enacted level but less than the Administration's request and the Senate committee and House bills. The difference was due in part to a $44.3 million reduction in the enacted level, apparently comprised of a $19.7 million general reduction and a $24.6 million "offset" for the centennial funding provided separately (see below) (Explanatory Statement, H16124-H16125). The FY2008 law agreed with the House in incorporating the Park Police account into the operations line item. See table 8.

Table 8. Appropriations for the National Park Service, FY2007-FY2008 ($ in millions)

National Park Service	FY2007 Approp.	FY2008 Request	FY2008 House	FY2008 Senate Comm.	FY2008 Approp.
Operation of the National Park System	1,848.4	2,057.1	2,047.8	2,046.8	1,970.6
— Park Management	*1,627.6*	*1,822.3*	*1,818.1*	*1,817.1*	*1,744.5*
— Administrative Costs	*135.1*	*146.7*	*141.6*	*141.6*	*139.4*
— U.S. Park Police	85.2	88.1	88.1	88.1	86.7
Centennial Challenge (Matching Prog.)	0.0	0.0[a]	50.0	0.0	24.6
National Recreation and Preservation[b]	54.4	48.9	62.9	68.5	67.4
Historic Preservation Fund[b]	65.7	63.7	81.5	75.0	70.4
Construction	297.5	201.6	201.6	227.2	218.4
Land and Water Conservation Fund[c]	-30.0	-30.0	-30.0	-30.0	-30.0
Land Acquisition and State Assistance	64.0	22.5	99.4	78.7	69.0
— Assistance to States	*29.6*	*0.0*	*50.0*	*30.0*	*24.6*
— NPS Acquisition	*34.4*	*22.5*	*49.4*	*48.7*	*44.4*
Total Appropriations	2,300.0[d]	2,363.8	2,513.2	2,461.4	2,390.3

a. The Administration requested the establishment of a mandatory fund with $100.0 million annually for ten years, to match nonfederal contributions to the NPS for certain purposes. The fund has not been authorized to date. This figure reflects that the Administration did not seek funding through annual appropriations.

b. For Preserve America, the Senate committee and the FY2008 appropriation reflect funding in the National Recreation and Preservation line item. The FY2007 appropriation, FY2008 request, and FY2008 House figures reflect Preserve America funds in Historic Preservation.

c. Figures reflect a rescission of contract authority.

d. Includes an emergency appropriation of $0.5 million not reflected in the figures above.

The majority of operations funding is provided directly to park managers. It supports the activities, programs, and services essential to the day-to-day operations of the park system, and covers resource protection, visitors' services, facility operations and maintenance, and park support programs, as well as such administrative expenses as employee pay, benefits, and other fixed costs. The FY2008 law provided $1.74 billion for park management, more than enacted for FY2007 but less than the House, Senate committee, and requested levels. The Administration, House, and Senate committee had sought relatively large increases for maintenance, visitor services, and resource stewardship.

United States Park Police (USPP)

The U.S. Park Police is an urban-oriented, full-service, uniformed law enforcement entity with primary jurisdiction at park sites within the metropolitan areas of Washington, DC, New York City, and San Francisco. USPP law enforcement authority extends to all NPS units and to certain other federal and state lands. The park police provide specialized law enforcement services to other park units when requested, through deployment of professional police officers to support law enforcement trained and commissioned park rangers working in park units system-wide. The FY2008 law provided $86.7 million, $1.5 million above FY2007. The House and Senate committee bills matched the request of $88.1 million. Increased funding was proposed primarily for enhanced security at National Mall icons, special events in Washington, DC, and at the Statue of Liberty in New York. As noted above, the FY2008 law moved the U.S. Park Police to the Operation of the National Park System line item.

Centennial Challenge

As discussed above, the Administration proposed a three-part National Parks Centennial Initiative, with additional funding for park operations (presumably included in the request for park management discussed above), donations, and federal funds to match the donations. The FY2008 law provided $24.6 million for a signature projects matching program. This is considered interim funding to initiate the program in 2008, and requires a 50:50 match. The House and Senate Appropriations Committees expressed an expectation that authorization will be enacted during the 110th Congress for a ten year program (Explanatory Statement, H16125). The House had approved $50.0 million to be available for matching donations in FY2008, while the Senate committee bill provided no money for the program. The Senate committee expressed support for the concept, but a preference that the authorizing committee address the issue (S.Rept. 110-91, p. 25). The President did not seek an annual appropriation for this purpose, but instead proposed the establishment of a mandatory program with $100.0 million annually for ten years. This program has not been authorized to date, and legislation would be required to effect this 10-year mandatory spending program.

National Recreation and Preservation

This line item funds a variety of park system recreation, natural and cultural resource protection programs, and an international park affairs office, as well as programs connected with state and local community efforts to preserve natural and historic resources. The FY2008 law provided $67.4 million, $18.5 million above the request and $13.0 million more than FY2007. The increase was partly the result of moving funding for Preserve America ($7.4 million) to this line item from Historic Preservation. Preserve America was funded at $4.9 million in FY2007, and the Senate committee originally supported $5.0 million. The Administration and the House had sought $10.0 million for FY2008.

The FY2008 appropriation included $15.3 million for the heritage partnership program that funds National Heritage Areas (NHAs). NHA funding was $5.3 million more than the request and $1.9 million above FY2007. For the statutory and contractual aid programs in specific, non-NPS sites, the FY2008 law allowed $7.5 million, $4.3 million more than FY2007. The Administration had proposed discontinuing statutory and contractual aid, as proposed (but not enacted) for FY2005-FY2007.

Construction

The construction line item funds new construction projects, as well as improvements, repair, rehabilitation, and replacement of park facilities. The FY2008 law provided $218.4 million for NPS construction, $79.1 million less than FY2007 and $8.8 million less than the Senate committee bill but $16.8 million more than the House approved and the Administration requested. Recent DOI data (March 2007) report an NPS deferred maintenance backlog of $7.9 billion, of which $4.3 billion is park roads, while another DOI source estimates an NPS backlog (midrange) of $9.1 billion for FY2006.

Land Acquisition and State Assistance

FY2008 appropriations for the NPS under the Land and Water Conservation Fund (LWCF) were $69.0 million, comprised of $44.4 million for NPS land acquisition and $24.6 million for state assistance programs. Land acquisition funds are used to acquire lands, or interests in lands, for inclusion within the National Park System. State assistance is for recreation-related land acquisition and recreation planning and development by the states, with the appropriated funds allocated by formula and states determining their spending priorities.

The $44.4 million for NPS land acquisition was $10.0 million above the FY2007 level and nearly double the Administration's request of $22.5 million. The House and Senate committee had sought higher funding levels. The Administration did not seek funds for state assistance from LWCF, requesting $1.4 million for program administration under National Recreation and Preservation. The $24.6 million for state assistance was $25.4 million less than the House, $5.4 million less than the Senate, and $5.0 million below the FY2007 enacted level. (For more information, see the "Land and Water Conservation Fund (LWCF)" section in this book.)

Historic Preservation

The Historic Preservation Fund (HPF), administered by the NPS, provides grants-in-aid for activities specified in the National Historic Preservation Act (NHPA; 16 U.S.C. §470), such as restoring historic districts, sites, buildings, and objects significant in American history and culture. NHPA reauthorization (P.L. 109-235) was enacted on December 22, 2006, and extends authority to fund the HPF through 2015. The Fund's preservation grants are normally funded on a 60% federal, 40% state matching share basis. The HPF also includes funding for *Save America's Treasures* grants.

The FY2008 law provided $70.4 million for the HPF, compared to an FY20007 amount of $65.7 million, representing a 7% increase. The FY2007 level included a $10.0 million hurricane recovery supplemental appropriation. The House and the Senate Appropriations Committee versions of the FY2008 funding bill would have provided $81.5 million and $75.0 million, respectively. The largest HPF activity, grants to state historic preservation offices, rose 6% from $37.2 million in FY2007 to $39.4 million for FY2008.

Additional funding was also provided for the *Save America's Treasures* and the *Preserve America* grant programs, which had been cut from $29.6 million in FY2006 to $13.0 million in FY2007. The FY2008 law provided $24.6 million for Save America's Treasures — triple the FY2007 level of $8.1 million, with over 55% of these funds allocated to congressionally-directed projects. While Preserve America funding also was increased, from $4.9 million to $7.4 million, the program was moved from the HPF to National Recreation and Preservation.

New for FY2008, the Park Service proposed to establish a $5.0 million program to help states and tribal governments create an integrated inventory of historic properties. Of that amount, $4.0 million would be to fund grants through the HPF and the balance would be provided through National Recreation and Preservation funding. This proposal was not funded.

For further information on the *National Park Service*, see its website at [http://www.nps.gov/].

For further information on *Historic Preservation*, see its website at [http://www.cr.nps.gov/hps/].

CRS Report RL33617. *Historic Preservation: Background and Funding,* by Susan Boren.

CRS Report RL33484. *National Park Management*, by Carol Hardy Vincent, Ross W. Gorte, Sandra L. Johnson, and Susan Boren.

CRS Report RL33525. *Recreation on Federal Lands*, coordinated by Kori Calvert and Carol Hardy Vincent.

U.S. GEOLOGICAL SURVEY

The U.S. Geological Survey (USGS) is the nation's premier science agency in providing physical and biological information related to natural hazards; certain aspects of the environment; and energy, mineral, water, and biological sciences. In addition, it is the federal government's principal civilian mapping agency and a primary source of data on the quality of the nation's water resources.

Funds for the USGS are provided in the line item *Surveys, Investigations, and Research*, for seven activities: Geographic Research, Investigations, and Remote Sensing; Geologic Hazards, Resources, and Processes; Water Resources Investigations; Biological Research; Enterprise Information; Science Support; and Facilities. The FY2008 law provided $1.01 billion for the USGS. This was the first time the USGS budget has been over a billion dollars. This amount was $31.5 million (3%) over the Administration's request of $975.0 million, and $18.4 million (2%) over the FY2007 enacted level of $988.1 million. See table 9.

Table 9. Appropriations for the U.S. Geological Survey, FY2007-FY2008 ($ in millions)

U.S. Geological Survey	FY2007 Approp.	FY2008 Request	FY2008 House Passed	FY2008 Senate Comm.	FY2008 Enacted
Enterprise Information	111.8	112.1	112.1	112.1	110.4
Geographic Research, Investigations, and Remote Sensing	80.2	75.0	80.0	78.5	77.7
Geologic Hazards, Resources, and Processes	237.0	222.1	249.8	243.3	243.5
Water Resources Investigations	214.9	212.5	223.5	224.1	220.5
Biological Research	175.7	181.1	187.1	182.1	179.9
Science Support	67.8	70.7[b]	68.7	68.2	67.2
Facilities	95.4	101.6	101.6	101.6	100.0
Global Climate Change Research	0.0	0.0	10.0	0.0	7.4
Total Appropriations	988.1[a]	975.0	1,032.8	1,009.9	1,006.5

a. The FY2007 total includes $5.3 million in P.L. 110-28.

b. This figure includes $2.4 million for the Financial and Business Management System. This amount was not included in the FY2008 law.

The FY2008 law provided $6.3 million for water resources research institutes and full funding for the mineral resource assessment program. Funding for these programs was not requested by the Administration. The law included an increase of $7.4 million for global climate change research, of which $2.5 million was directed to establish the National Global Warming and Wildlife Science Center.

Enterprise Information

In FY2005, the Administration proposed a new line item for funding within the USGS called Enterprise Information. This program consolidates funding of all USGS information needs including information technology, security, services, and resources management, as well as capital asset planning. The FY2008 law provided 110.4 million for Enterprise Information, which was $1.7 million below the Administration's request of $112.1 million and $1.4 million below the FY2007 level of $111.8 million.

There are three primary programs within Enterprise Information: (1) enterprise information security and technology, which supports management and operations of USGS telecommunications (e.g., computing infrastructure and email); (2) enterprise information resources, which provides policy support, information management, and oversight over information services; and (3) national geospatial program, which provides operational support and management for the Federal Geographic Data committee (FGDC). The FGDC is an interagency, intergovernmental committee that encourages collaboration to make geospatial data available to state, local, and tribal governments, as well as communities.

Geographic Research, Investigations, and Remote Sensing

This program aims to provide access to high quality geospatial information to the public.

The FY2008 law provided $77.7 million for this program, which was $2.8 million above the Administration's request of $75.0 million, and $2.5 million below the FY2007 level of $80.2 million. Under the Land Remote Sensing subheading, $24.2 million was requested to support the Landsat Data Continuity Mission, also known as Landsat 8. Landsat 8 is an upcoming satellite that is to take remotely sensed images of the Earth's land surface and surrounding coastal areas primarily for environmental monitoring. The volume of data taken by Landsat 8 is to be four times greater than its predecessor, Landsat 7, and Landsat 8 is to include additional spectral bands and higher resolution than Landsat 7 data. The FY2008 law appeared to support the requested funding level for Landsat 8. The Senate recommendation for a priority ecosystem restoration program was not included in the FY2008 law.

Geologic Hazards, Resources, and Processes

For Geologic Hazards, Resources, and Processes activities, the FY2008 law provided $243.5 million, which is $21.4 million above the Administration's request, and $6.5 million about the FY2007 level. This line item covers programs in three activities: Hazard Assessments, Landscape and Coastal Assessments, and Resource Assessments.

The primary reduction sought by the Administration was a $20.1 million cut in the mineral resources program. According to the Administration, universities or other entities will undertake assessments and research that support nonfederal needs. In previous years the Administration requested similar cuts in this program, yet each year funding was provided. The FY2008 law reinstated funding for this program and the Appropriations Committees referred to the Administration's request as irresponsible (Explanatory Statement, H16128).

The FY2008 law contained $85.7 million for the geologic hazards program, $1.6 million above the Administration's request. Some of the funds would go towards supporting research and monitoring on volcanoes, landslides, and earthquakes. The joint explanatory statement states Congress's strong support for the multi-hazard initiative.

Water Resources Investigations

The FY2008 law provided $220.5 million for Water Resources Investigations, which was $8.1 million above the Administration's request of $212.5 million, and $5.6 million above the FY2007 level of $214.9 million. As with the Bush Administration's FY2002-FY2007 budget requests, the FY2008 request had sought to discontinue USGS support for water resources research institutes because, according to the Administration, most institutes have succeeded in leveraging sufficient funding for program activities from non-USGS sources. Nevertheless, the institutes received funding from FY2002-FY2007, with $5.4 million appropriated for FY2007. The FY2008 law provided $6.3 million.

The FY2008 law provided $20.1 million for the National Streamflow Information Program (NSIP), an increase of $3.5 million over the FY2007 enacted level. Funds would be used to continue the operation of the streamgage network of 7,400 streamgages. Further, they would allow for several new streamgages to be built and maintained. Through the NSIP, the USGS collects the streamflow data needed by federal, state, and local agencies for planning, operating water-resources projects, and regulatory programs.

Biological Research

The Biological Research Program under the USGS generates and distributes information related to conserving and managing the nation's biological resources. The FY2008 law provided 179.9 million for the program, $1.2 million below the Administration's request of $181.1 million and $4.2 million above the FY2007 level of $175.7 million.

In cooperation with the FWS and other federal and state agencies, the USGS is surveying for the early detection of avian flu in wild birds, and collecting samples from birds that are known to migrate through the Russian Far East and Southeast Asia. For 2008, the USGS will continue sampling birds for avian flu and coordinate with other agencies to address the potential for avian flu in North America.

Science Support and Facilities

Science Support focuses on those costs associated with modernizing the infrastructure for managing and disseminating scientific information. The FY2008 law provided $67.2 million for Science Support, a decrease of $3.5 million from the Administration's request of $70.7 million and decrease of $0.6 million from the FY2007 level of $67.8 million

Facilities focuses on the costs for maintenance and repair. The FY2008 law provided $100.0 million for Facilities, which is $1.6 million below the Administration's request and an increase of $4.5 million above the FY2007 enacted level of $95.4 million.

For further information on the *U.S. Geological Survey*, see its website at [http://www.usgs.gov/].

Minerals Management Service

The Minerals Management Service (MMS) administers two programs: the Offshore Minerals Management (OMM) Program and the Minerals Revenue Management (MRM) Program. OMM administers competitive leasing on Outer Continental Shelf (OCS) lands and oversees production of offshore oil, gas, other minerals, and offshore alternative energy. MRM collects and disburses bonuses, rents, and royalties paid on federal onshore and OCS leases and Indian mineral leases. Revenues from onshore leases are distributed to states in which they were collected, the general fund of the U.S. Treasury, and designated programs. Revenues from the offshore leases are allocated among the coastal states, the Land and Water Conservation Fund, the Historic Preservation Fund, and the U.S. Treasury.

The MMS collected and disbursed about $11.5 billion in revenue in FY2007 from mineral leases on federal and Indian lands. This amount fluctuates annually based primarily on the prices of oil and natural gas. Over the past decade, royalties from natural gas production have accounted for 40% to 45% of annual MMS receipts, while oil royalties have been not more than 25%. However, in FY2007, oil royalties accounted for about 38.5% of MMS receipts. Other sources of MMS receipts include rents and bonuses for all leaseable minerals and royalties from coal and other minerals.

Budget and Appropriations

The FY2008 funding level for MMS was $294.7 million, composed of: $115.9 million in appropriations; $135.7 million in offsetting collections, which MMS has been retaining since 1994; and $43.0 million in state cost sharing deductions, as had been proposed by the House. This would be an increase of $6.4 million (2%) over the total funding of $288.2 million in FY2007. The Senate Appropriations Committee had recommended a total MMS budget of $302.1 million, consisting of a $166.4 million appropriation and $135.7 million in offsetting collections. The House had approved a total of $295.7 million, but much less funding through the annual appropriation process. Specifically, the House had included $67.0 million in appropriations, $135.7 million in offsetting collections, and an "administrative provisions" section resulting in a $50.0 million deferral for ultra deepwater research and a $43.0 million deduction for state royalty administrative costs. See table 10.

Table 10. Appropriations for the Minerals Management Service, FY2007-FY2008 ($ in millions)

Minerals Management Service	FY2007 Approp.	FY2008 Request	FY2008 House Passed	FY2008 Senate Comm.	FY2008 Approp.
Royalty and Offshore Minerals Management					
— OCS Lands (OMM)	*152.8*	*160.0*	*159.0*	*164.9*	*160.1*
— Royalty Management (MRM)	*80.1*	*82.4*	*82.4*	*82.4*	*81.1*
— General Administration	*48.5*	*48.5*	*48.0*	*48.5*	*47.2*
— Gross, Royalty and Offshore Minerals Management	*281.3*	*290.8*	*289.3*	*295.7*	*288.4*
— Use of Receipts	*-128.7*	*-135.7*	*-135.7*	*-135.7*	*-135.7*
Total, Royalty and Offshore Minerals Management Appropriations	152.6	155.0	153.6	159.9	152.6
Oil Spill Research	6.9	6.4	6.4	6.4	6.3
Administrative Provisions					
— Ultra Deepwater Research Deferral	—	—	-50.0	—	— -
— State Royalty Administrative Cost Deduction	—	—	-43.0	—	-43.0
Total Appropriations	159.5	161.5	67.0	166.4	115.9

The FY2008 appropriations law included House-passed language regarding state royalty administrative costs. The law required the Secretary of the Interior to deduct 2% from the states' 50% share of revenue from onshore federal leases for FY2008. Congress established net receipts sharing in 1991, which required states to pay for a portion of the administrative costs associated with managing federal leases in their states. In 2000, P.L. 106-393 ended that requirement and allowed states to receive their full share of revenue from federal leases within their state.

The FY2008 appropriations law did not include other House-passed language to prevent transfers of funds into the Ultra-Deepwater and Unconventional Natural Gas and Other Petroleum Research Fund (the Fund). The Fund was created as a mandatory program in the Energy Policy Act of 2005 (P.L. 109-58) and was authorized to receive $50 million each year from FY2007-FY2017 from federal oil and gas leasing receipts. The Administration had proposed both to repeal the Fund and reintroduce net receipts sharing among states. The House-passed bill reflected support for the Administration's proposals through *scoring credits*, resulting in a $50.0 million deferral for ultra deepwater research as well as the $43.0 million deduction for state royalty administrative costs. See table 10.

Oil and Gas Leasing Offshore

Issues not directly tied to specific funding accounts remain controversial. Oil and gas development moratoria in the OCS along the Atlantic and Pacific Coasts, parts of Alaska, and the Gulf of Mexico have been in place since 1982, as a result of public laws and executive orders of the President. However, Congress enacted separate legislation (P.L. 109-432) to open part of the Gulf of Mexico (about 5.8 million acres) previously under the moratoria, but the law places nearly all of the eastern Gulf under a leasing moratorium until 2022. The law also contains revenue sharing provisions for selected coastal states. Two areas —Bristol Bay (AK) and Virginia — contained in the MMS Proposed Final Five-Year OCS Oil and Gas Leasing Program (2007-2012) remain controversial. Bristol Bay was removed from the congressional moratoria, while oil and gas leasing off Virginia remains under the moratoria. The new five-year program took effect July 1, 2007.

The FY2008 appropriations law did not contain House-passed language barring funds in the bill from being used for new leases for those holding leases under the Deep Water Royalty Relief Act of 1995 without price thresholds. The Appropriations Committees expressed continued commitment to this issue and the expectation that the authorizing committees would complete action on this matter (Explanatory Statement, H16130). The Senate Appropriations Committee had rejected bill language that would have prohibited the government from issuing new offshore leases to companies holding deepwater leases without price thresholds.

Royalty relief for OCS oil and gas producers also was debated during consideration of FY2007 Interior appropriations. On February 13, 2006, the *New York Times* reported that the MMS would not collect royalties on leases awarded in 1998 and 1999 because no price threshold was included in the lease agreements during those two years. Without the price thresholds, producers may produce oil and gas up to specified volumes without paying royalties no matter what the price. The MMS asserts that placing price thresholds in the lease agreements is at the discretion of the Secretary of the

Interior. However, according to the MMS, the price thresholds were omitted by mistake during 1998 and 1999.[8]

On January 18, 2007, the House passed a bill (H.R. 6) that would deny new Gulf of Mexico leases to those holding leases without price thresholds or payment or an agreement to pay a "conservation of resources" fee that would be established by H.R. 6. DOI has asserted that the House-passed bill could lead to legal challenges which could delay oil and gas development in the Gulf of Mexico. The Department also suggested that Congress offer the lessees a three-year extension to their leases as an incentive to amend the leases to include price thresholds. The House-passed language was not enacted in the Energy Independence and Security Act of 2007 (P.L. 110-140).[9]

During consideration of FY2008 Interior appropriations, the House considered other amendments related to the OCS. An amendment which would have lifted the OCS moratoria for natural gas leasing and development beyond 25 miles from the coastline was defeated. Related amendments to open the OCS for oil and gas drilling beyond 100 miles of the coastline and to open the entire OCS currently under the moratoria were defeated.

For FY2008, the Appropriations Committees provided direction related to drilling in the North Aleutian Basin Planning Area, also known as Bristol Bay (Explanatory Statement, H16128). They expressed that drilling in that area should be conducted only after the availability of detailed studies and information. They directed MMS and other scientific bodies to document oil spill containment and responses to accidents. Further, the MMS was required to complete a 2 1/2 - 3 year pre-sale and NEPA process including the preparation of an Environmental Impact Statement before proceeding with the North Aleutian Basin sale.

Another challenge confronting the MMS is to ensure that its audit and compliance program is consistently effective. Critics contend that less auditing and more focus on compliance review has led to a less rigorous royalty collection system and thus a loss of revenue to the federal Treasury. DOI's Inspector General (IG) has made recommendations to strengthen and improve administrative controls of the Compliance and Asset Management Program (CAM). Further, DOI established an independent panel to review the MMS Mineral Leasing Program. The review included an examination of the Royalty-in-Kind Program which has grown significantly over the past three years — from 41.5 million barrels of oil equivalent (BOE) sold in 2004 to 112 million BOE sold in 2007.[10] The House Appropriations Committee, in report language on the FY2008 bill, expressed concern about IG reports on the need for more and better audits, and directed MMS to report on corrective actions it is taking (H.Rept. 110-187, p. 58).

Oil and gas leasing in offshore California also has continued to be a controversial issue. Under the Coastal Zone Management Act of 1972, as amended (16 U.S.C. §1451-64) (CZMA), development of federal offshore leases must be consistent with state coastal zone management plans. In 1999, MMS extended the terms of 36 leases in offshore California by granting suspensions of the leases' five-year terms. A suspension extends the term of the lease, to allow the lessee to facilitate development.[11] The state of California sued, contending that MMS should have made a consistency determination showing that the lease suspensions were consistent with California's coastal management plan before issuing the suspensions. In June 2001, the U.S. Court for the Northern District of California agreed with the state of California and struck down the lease suspensions.[12] MMS appealed to the U.S. Court of Appeals for the Ninth Circuit. However, in December 2002, the Ninth Circuit upheld the District Court decision.[13]

Following this ruling, nine oil company lessees brought breach of contract claims against MMS seeking restitution for "bonus payments" made to MMS in order to obtain and suspend their leases in offshore California. In November 2005, the U.S. Court of Federal Claims held that the federal government breached its contract with the lessees when it enacted the amendments to the CZMA in 1990 that, according to the decisions described above, required lease suspensions to be evaluated for consistency with a state's coastal management plan.[14] The Court reasoned that the lessees had not bargained for the more extensive consistency determination requirements to be applied to suspension requests when the leases were signed, and that therefore the legislation creating these new requirements amounted to breach of the leases.[15] The government was ordered to repay the lessees for all so-called "bonus payments" made to the government in exchange for the leases.[16]

For further information on the *Minerals Management Service*, see its website at [http://www.mms.gov].

CRS Report RL33974. Legal Issues Raised by Provision in House Energy Bill (H.R. 6) Creating Incentives for Certain OCS Leaseholders to Accept Price Thresholds, by Robert Meltz and Adam Vann.

CRS Report RL33493. Outer Continental Shelf: Debate Over Oil and Gas Leasing and Revenue Sharing, by Marc Humphries.

CRS Report RS22567. Royalty Relief for U.S. Deepwater Oil and Gas Leases, by Marc Humphries.

OFFICE OF SURFACE MINING RECLAMATION AND ENFORCEMENT

The Surface Mining Control and Reclamation Act of 1977 (SMCRA, P.L. 95-87; 30 U.S.C. §1201 note) established the Office of Surface Mining Reclamation and Enforcement (OSM) to ensure that land mined for coal would be returned to a condition capable of supporting its pre-mining land use. However, coal mining is an old activity in the United States, and at the time SMCRA was enacted there was a large inventory of abandoned mine sites that no company could be held accountable to reclaim. To address this problem, SMCRA established an Abandoned Mine Land (AML) fund, with fees levied on coal production, to reclaim abandoned sites that posed serious health or safety hazards. The law provided that individual states and Indian tribes would develop their own regulatory programs incorporating minimum standards established by law and regulations. Reclamation in states with no approved programs is directed by OSM.

Historically, AML collections have been divided up and assigned to different accounts, some of which fall into a federal designation allocated to individual states based upon their ranking in historical coal production. A portion of fee collections also has been credited to a state share account. Grants to states and tribes for reclamation have been awarded after applying a formula to annual congressional appropriations from the AML fund. Grants to a state or tribe would draw on both that state's federal-share and state-share accounts. Collections have exceeded appropriations for a number of years. The total unappropriated balance — including both federal and state share accounts in the AML fund — was over $1.95 billion by the end of FY2006, of which approximately $1.2 billion was in the state-share accounts.

As coal production has shifted westward, western states have paid more into the fund. These states have contended that they are shouldering a disproportionate share of the reclamation burden because the great majority of the sites requiring remediation are in the East.[17] Several states were pressing for increases in the AML appropriations, with an eye on those unappropriated balances in the state-share accounts.

The Tax Relief and Health Care Act (P.L. 109-432) reauthorized AML fee collections through FY2021, and also made significant changes in the procedures for disbursing grants. Grants will be funded by permanent appropriations from the AML fund and the general fund of the U. S. Treasury. All the revenues paid to the fund during a given fiscal year will be returned during the fiscal year that follows.[18] Under the restructuring, the balances in the state- and tribal-share accounts will be returned to all states and tribes in seven annual installments paid with general Treasury funds.[19]

States and tribes are categorized as "Certified" or "Uncertified," and distributions to each differ. Certified states are those that have reclaimed the most serious sites, while uncertified states have not yet done so. Beginning in FY2008, and over a period of seven years, certified states will receive equal installments of the unappropriated balances in their state-share accounts as of the end of FY2006. Additionally, they will receive whatever grants they would be entitled to based upon application of the distribution formula to both prior year collections and that state's entitlement based upon its historic coal production.[20] Beginning with fees collected during FY2008, the amounts that would have been deposited to certified states' state-share accounts will instead be credited to the federal-share account representing historical coal production. Certified states will not receive this allocation in their annual grants after FY2008. This is intended to have the effect of increasing the pool of money available for distribution to uncertified states in future years.

The level of grants distributed to uncertified states will be based upon their proportionate entitlement from the historical coal production account (which, as just noted, will hold more money than under the old system), as well as the amount that would have otherwise been deposited to the state-share account.[21]

Owing to the establishment of the permanent appropriation, the FY2008 OSM budget request was sharply lower than the FY2007 level. Overall, the FY2008 budget request for OSM totaled $168.3 million in discretionary spending, a reduction of $126.3 million (43%) from the FY2007 level of $294.6 million. However, due to the restructuring of the program to provide for repayment of the unappropriated state balances from Treasury funds, one cannot make a direct comparison between the FY2007 appropriated level for OSM and the FY2008 levels.

In FY2008, some activities will remain subject to annual appropriations. Among these are the expenses of federal AML programs in states with no OSM-approved reclamation programs, an emergency reclamation program, OSM administrative expenses, and the Clean Streams program. The agency budget also has an additional component — regulatory and technology programs.

The FY2008 appropriations law provided a total of $118.5 million for Regulation and Technology and $52.0 million for the AML fund. The total appropriation of $170.4 million for the Office of Surface Mining is roughly $2.1 million (1%) higher than the Administration's request.

As is summarized in table 11, there was, in fact, no wide disparity in the funding levels recommended by the House and the Senate committee on Appropriations. The House had approved a $1.9 million boost to Regulation and Technology, an addition of 2%, over the Administration's request for $115.5 million. The additional funds were intended for environmental protection activities. The Senate Appropriations Committee recommended $121.5 million, an increase of $6.0 million above the Administration's request. The increase was to include additional funds to match state costs for the conduct of regulatory programs intended to minimize impacts of coal extraction on local environments and populations. Both the full House and the Senate Appropriations Committee agreed with the Administration request of $52.8 million for AML. In total, the House approved $170.2 million for OSM, $1.9 million (1%) over the Administration's request and $124.5 million (42%) below FY2007. The Senate Committee on Appropriations recommended a total of $174.3 million for OSM, $6.0 million (4%) over the Administration's request and $120.3 million (41%) below FY2007.

Table 11. Appropriations for the Office of Surface Mining Reclamation and Enforcement, FY2007-FY2008 ($ in millions)

Office of Surface Mining Reclamation and Enforcement	FY2007 Approp.	FY2008 Request	FY2008 House Passed	FY2008 Senate Comm.	FY2008 Approp.
Regulation and Technology	109.2	115.5	117.3	121.5	118.5
— Environmental Protection	78.7	83.8	85.9	89.8	87.4
Abandoned Mine Reclamation Fund	185.4	52.8	52.8	52.8	52.0
Total Appropriations	294.6	168.3	170.2	174.3	170.4

For further information on the *Office of Surface Mining Reclamation and Enforcement*, see its website at [http://www.osmre.gov/osm.htm].

CRS Report RL32993. Abandoned Mine Reclamation Fee on Coal, by Nonna A. Noto.

BUREAU OF INDIAN AFFAIRS

The Bureau of Indian Affairs (BIA) provides a variety of services to federally recognized American Indian and Alaska Native tribes and their members, and historically has been the lead agency in federal dealings with tribes. Programs provided or funded through the BIA include government operations, courts, law enforcement, fire protection, social programs, education, roads, economic development, employment assistance, housing repair, dams, Indian rights protection, implementation of land and water settlements, management of trust assets (real estate and natural resources), and partial gaming oversight.

BIA's direct appropriations were $2.31 billion in FY2007. For FY2008, the Consolidated Appropriations Act provided $2.29 billion for the BIA, a decrease of $17.0 million (1%) from FY2007. The Administration had proposed $2.23 billion for FY2008, the House had approved $2.35 billion, and the Senate Appropriations Committee had recommended $2.27 billion. The FY2008 enacted amount for the BIA was $62.4 million (3%) more than the Administration's proposal, $55.7 million (2%) less than the House amount, and $25.6 million (1%) more than the Senate committee's recommendation. See table 12 for more detailed BIA appropriations figures.

Key issues for the BIA include education programs — including the Administration's proposals to increase education management spending, eliminate funding for the Johnson-O'Malley program and tribal technical colleges, and reduce education construction — as well as BIA law enforcement and housing programs, and the Interior Department's process for acknowledging Indian tribes.

Bureau of Indian Education (BIE) Programs[22]

BIE funds an elementary-secondary school system and higher education programs. The BIE school system comprises 184 BIE-funded schools and peripheral dormitories, with over 2,000 structures, educating about 46,000 students in 23 states. Tribes and tribal organizations, under self-determination contracts and other grants, operate 123 of these institutions; the BIE operates the remainder. The BIE operates two postsecondary schools and provides grants to 26 tribally controlled colleges and two tribally controlled technical colleges. Key problems for the BIE-funded school system are low student achievement, the high proportion of schools failing to make adequate yearly progress (AYP), and the large number of inadequate school facilities.

Table 12. Appropriations for the Bureau of Indian Affairs, FY2007-FY2008 ($ in thousands)

Bureau of Indian Affairs	FY2007 Approp.	FY2008 Request	FY2008 House Passed	FY2008 Senate Comm.	FY2008 Approp.
Operation of Indian Programs					
Tribal Government	392,261	397,698	403,009	406,398	399,862
— Johnson-O'Malley Grants[a]	7,700	0	5,311	7,700	N/A
— Housing Improvement Program[b]	4,266	0	0	0	N/A
— Contract Support Costs	143,628	149,628	149,628	149,628	147,294
Human Services	144,824	120,703	146,548	134,128	139,339
— Welfare Assistance	80,179	74,164	80,179	77,164	78,928
— Housing Improvement Program[b]	18,824	0	18,830	9,425	13,614
Trust - Natural Resources Management	145,238	141,684	152,684	147,489	147,157
Trust - Real Estate Services	144,073	150,722	150,722	151,722	148,371
— Probate	15,884	19,883	19,883	19,883	N/A
— Real Estate Services	43,510	47,964	47,964	48,964	N/A
— Land Records Improvement	7,897	16,065	16,065	16,065	N/A
Bureau of Indian Education	657,912	660,540	699,040	685,540	689,611
— Elementary/ Secondary (Forward- Funded)	458,310	476,500	487,500	476,500	479,895
— Elementary/ Secondary [Other]	60,390	61,803	61,803	69,803	74,620
— Johnson-O'Malley Grants[a]	12,000	0	16,500	8,000	N/A
— Post Secondary Programs	108,619	98,520	109,520	115,520	111,749
— Tribal Colleges and Universities	54,721	54,721	54,721	59,721	N/A
— Tribal Colls. and Univs. Supplements to Grants[c]	4,588	1,292	1,292	1,292	N/A

Table 12. (Continued).

Bureau of Indian Affairs	FY2007 Approp.	FY2008 Request	FY2008 House Passed	FY2008 Senate Comm.	FY2008 Approp.
— Tribal Technical Colleges[c]	2,004	0	6,000	6,000	N/A
— Education Management	18,593	23,717	23,717	23,717	23,347
Public Safety and Justice	217,611	233,818	250,018	237,818	243,657
— Law Enforcement	204,454	221,753	231,753	225,753	228,138
— Detention/Corrections	58,678	65,038	65,038	67,038	N/A
— Tribal Courts	12,013	12,065	17,065	12,065	14,338
Community and Economic Development	42,234	39,061	47,339	39,061	39,436
Executive Direction and Administrative Services	244,070	246,692	244,185	244,185	240,376
— Office of Federal Acknowledgment	1,900	1,900	2,900	1,900	N/A
— Information Resources Technology	53,199	53,704	53,704	53,704	N/A
Subtotal, Operation of Indian Programs	1,988,2 23	1,990,918	2,093,545	2,046,341	2,047,809
Construction					
Education Construction	204,956	139,844	145,200	125,029	142,935
— Replacement School Construction	83,891	14,815	14,815	0	N/A
— Replacement Facility Construction	26,873	22,578	22,578	22,578	N/A
— Education Facilities Improvement and Repair	92,219	100,834	105,834	100,834	N/A
Public Safety and Justice Construction	11,605	11,621	14,621	11,621	14,393
— Law Enforcement Facilities Improvement and Repair	8,103	8,111	11,111	8,111	N/A

Table 12. (Continued).

Bureau of Indian Affairs	FY2007 Approp.	FY2008 Request	FY2008 House Passed	FY2008 Senate Comm.	FY2008 Approp.
Resources Management Construction	45,125	37,916	39,916	37,916	38,309
General Administration Construction and Construction Management	10,137	8,246	8,246	8,246	N/A
Subtotal, Construction	271,823	197,627	207,983	179,012[d]	203,754
Land and Water Claim Settlements and Miscellaneous Payments	42,000	34,069	39,136	34,069	33,538
Indian Guaranteed Loan Program	6,258	6,276	6,276	6,276	6,178

Note: N/A = Not available.

[a] The Johnson O'Malley program is split between two budget activities, Tribal Government and Bureau of Indian Education.

[b]. The Housing Improvement Program is split between two budget activities, Tribal Government and Human Services.

[c]. Of the FY2007 amount for Tribal Colleges and Universities Supplements to Grants, $3.3 million is for tribal technical colleges.

[d]. Reflects a rescission of $3.8 million of unobligated prior year balances.

Proposed Indian Education Initiative

The Administration proposed a nearly $15-million initiative in FY2008 to enhance education at BIE-funded schools. BIE's forward-funded elementary and secondary budget activity would receive $9.6 million of the new program funds; these funds would be used to improve instructional resources (especially through teacher development and principal training) at BIE schools being restructured to meet AYP goals ($5.3 million), and to increase operation and maintenance funds for student transportation ($4.3 million). The remaining $5.3 million of the initiative would go to BIE's education management budget activity, to add education and administrative specialists at education line offices ($4.0 million) and maintain BIE's new student and school information system ($1.2 million). Both the full House and the Senate

Appropriations Committee approved these initiatives, but the House approved an additional $7.0 million for meeting AYP goals and an additional $1.0 million for student transportation. The amount of appropriations enacted for FY2008 for the education initiative is being determined through the OMB report under §437 of the Interior portion of the Consolidated Appropriations Act.

Johnson-O'Malley (JOM) Program

The JOM program provides supplementary education assistance grants for tribes and public schools to benefit Indian students, and is funded in two budget activities, Tribal Government and BIE. In FY2007, JOM was funded at $7.7 million in the Tribal Government activity and $12.0 million in the BIE activity. The Administration proposed no funding for this program in FY2008, asserting that Department of Education programs under Titles I (education of the disadvantaged) and VII (Indian education) of the Elementary and Secondary Education Act[23] provide funds for the same purposes, and that the funds should be used for BIE-funded schools. Opponents disagree that the Education Department programs can replace what they see as JOM's culturally relevant programs. The House Appropriations Committee rejected the Administration's proposal to end JOM funding in FY2008, stating that the Administration's argument has not been substantiated (H.Rept. 110-187, p. 70). For FY2008, the House approved $5.3 million under Tribal Government and $16.5 million under BIE for JOM. The Senate committee recommended $7.7 million under Tribal Government and $8.0 million under BIE. The amount enacted for JOM by the Consolidated Appropriations Act, under the Tribal Government budget activity, is being determined through the OMB report under §437. The act's explanatory statement specified $14.0 million for JOM under BIE, before an across-the-board rescission of 1.56% for discretionary programs.

Tribal Technical Colleges

There are two tribal technical (or vocational) colleges, one in North Dakota (United Tribes Technical College) and one on the Navajo Reservation (Navajo Technical College, formerly Crownpoint Institute of Technology). Both colleges are statutorily excluded from the BIE tribal colleges and universities assistance program,[24] but the two are the only colleges receiving grants under the Education Department's Carl Perkins Act program for tribally controlled vocational colleges.[25] The BIE has for several years sought to end its funding for the two technical colleges, asserting that they receive adequate funding from the Perkins Act and other

Education Department higher education programs and that the funds are needed more at the 26 tribal colleges and universities. Congress has not agreed to the Administration's recommendation. The tribal technical colleges received a total of $5.3 million in FY2007, split between the BIA's Community Development budget activity and the BIE's Post Secondary Programs budget subactivity. The Administration proposed no funding for tribal technical colleges in FY2008, but neither the full House nor the Senate committee agreed. The House approved, and the Senate committee recommended, $6.0 million for tribal technical colleges, all in the BIE Post Secondary Programs budget subactivity. The explanatory statement on the FY2008 Act agreed, specifying $6.0 million for the two tribal technical colleges (without the rescission).

Education Construction

Many BIE school facilities are old and dilapidated, with health and safety deficiencies. BIA education construction covers both construction of new school facilities to replace facilities that cannot be repaired, and improvement and repair of existing facilities. Schools are replaced or repaired according to priority lists. Table 12 shows education construction funds. For FY2008, the Administration had proposed reducing the appropriation for education construction by $65.1 million (32%). Included was a reduction of $69.1 million (82%) for construction of replacement schools, leaving $14.8 million for two new replacement schools. The Administration asserted that construction and repairs since 2001 have reduced the proportion of BIE facilities in bad condition from about 66% to 31%, and that the BIA needed to focus on completing replacement schools funded in prior years. Opponents of a reduction contend that a large proportion of BIA schools still need replacement or major repairs and thus funding should not be cut.

The FY2008 appropriations law supported a significant reduction for education construction. It contained the House-passed level of $145.2 million, reduced to $142.9 million after the rescission. This was a reduction of $62.0 million (30%) from the FY2007 level of $205.0 million. The amounts enacted for replacement school construction and other education construction activities are being determined through the OMB report under §437. The act's explanatory statement also approved the BIE plan to complete existing school construction and alleviate current construction shortfalls before beginning new school construction projects. While the House had approved $145.2 million for education construction, the Senate Appropriations Committee had recommended $125.0 million. The Senate committee had recommended no funding for replacement school construction, stating that the BIA informed them that 15 replacement school construction projects (of 18 total) had funding shortfalls, totaling $143 million overall, and that the Committee believed it imprudent to start new projects until the BIA presented a plan to address the shortfalls (S.Rept. 110-91, p. 39).

Law Enforcement Program

BIA and Justice Department figures show rising crime rates, methamphetamine use, and juvenile gang activity on some Indian reservations. The federal government has lead jurisdiction over major criminal offenses on most Indian reservations, although in some states federal law has transferred criminal jurisdiction to the state. Tribes share jurisdiction but under federal law tribal courts have limited sentencing options. In general, tribes have fewer law enforcement resources. The BIA funds most law enforcement, jails, and courts in Indian country, whether operated by tribes or the BIA. For FY2008 the Administration proposed a "Safe Indian Communities Initiative" involving a $17.3 million total increase (8%) in BIA law enforcement funding, to $221.8 million. Included in the initiative were $5.4 million for additional officers, equipment, and training; $6.4 million to increase staffing at detention and corrections facilities, a need identified in a 2004 Interior Inspector General report; and $5.4 million for specialized drug enforcement training, especially regarding methamphetamine. Indian tribes and supporters, estimating a 42% shortfall in law enforcement staffing, suggested the Administration's initiative was insufficient for adequate policing on reservations[26] and may not have been sufficient to handle the methamphetamine problem.

For BIA law enforcement, the FY2008 appropriations law included the House-passed level of $231.8 million, reduced to $228.1 million after the rescission. This was a $23.7 million increase (12%) over the FY2007 level of $204.5 million. The amounts enacted for specific activities are being determined through the OMB report under §437. The Appropriations Committees directed the BIA to use all available existing authorities to increase law enforcement and criminal prosecutions, and to allocate the funding increases for tribal law enforcement outside the usual methodology in order to serve areas with the greatest need, especially remote reservations.

The House total of $231.8 million included $9.5 million over the Administration's request to combat methamphetamine abuse. The Senate

Appropriations Committee had recommended $225.8 million for BIA law enforcement. The Committee did not include funds specifically for methamphetamine abuse, but instead increased funding for criminal investigations and for detention/corrections by $2.0 million each over the requested and House-approved amounts. The Senate committee also required the BIA to report on the needs of BIA- and tribally operated detention facilities for staffing, operation and maintenance, and improvement and repairs (S.Rept. 110-91, p. 38).

For tribal courts, the FY2008 appropriations law provided $14.3 million, which was a $2.3 million (19%) increase over the FY2007 level of $12.0 million. The Administration had proposed a small increase (0.4%), to $12.1 million, while Indian tribes and supporters urged greater funding. The House had approved $17.1 million for tribal courts, while the Senate committee had recommended $12.1 million.

Housing Improvement Program (HIP)

The major federal Indian housing program is the Indian Housing Block Grant administered by the Department of Housing and Urban Development (HUD), which funds all types of housing. BIA's HIP, an older and much smaller program, focuses on urgently needed repairs, renovations, or modest new houses, on or near reservations, especially for the neediest families. BIA has considered HIP a safety net for those not eligible for or not served by the HUD program. Total HIP funding was $23.1 million in FY2007, split between the Tribal Government budget activity ($4.3 million) and the Human Services activity ($18.8 million). The Administration proposed eliminating HIP for FY2008, contending that its recipients are not statutorily barred from the HUD program, that it serves a limited number of tribes, and that other BIA programs are of higher priority. Indian tribes and supporters opposed the elimination of HIP, asserting that HIP meets a great need for rehabilitation of substandard housing, and questioning whether the HUD program could fill the need for urgent housing repairs.

The FY2008 appropriations law contained $13.6 million for HIP for FY2008. The House had declined to end HIP, approving $18.8 million in FY2008 in the Human Services budget activity only, a slight increase ($6,000, or less than 1%) from the FY2007 Human Services portion, but a decrease of $4.3 million from total HIP funding in FY2007. The House Appropriations Committee directed the BIA and HUD to evaluate HIP's effectiveness and determine whether HIP and its eligibility criteria could be integrated into existing HUD programs (H.Rept. 110-187, p. 69). The Senate Appropriations Committee had recommended $9.4 million for HIP.

Federal Tribal Acknowledgment Process

Federal recognition brings an Indian tribe unique benefits, including partial sovereignty, jurisdictional powers, and eligibility for federal Indian programs. Tribes have been acknowledged in many ways, but it was not until 1978 that the Interior Department established a regulatory process for acknowledgment decisions (25 CFR 83).[27] First located within the BIA, the recognition office is now in the office of the Assistant Secretary — Indian Affairs, as the Office of Federal Acknowledgment (OFA). OFA employs teams of expert ethnohistorians, genealogists, and anthropologists to consider recognition petitions. The OFA process has been frequently criticized for taking too long, one reason for which is a lack of resources.[28] For FY2007, OFA received $1.9 million within the Executive Direction budget activity, which funds the Assistant Secretary's office. The Administration requested, and the Senate committee recommended, the same amount for FY2008. The House approved an amendment to designate an additional $1.0 million for OFA in FY2008, bringing OFA's total to $2.9 million within the Assistant Secretary's office. The House's goal was to add several teams of experts to increase the number of decisions on recognition petitions. The FY2008 appropriations law provided $240.4 million for the Executive Direction budget activity, within which OFA is funded, but the specific amount for OFA is being determined through the OMB report under §437.

For further information on education programs of the *Bureau of Indian Education*, see its website at [http://www.oiep.bia.edu].

CRS Report RL34205. Federal Indian Education Programs: Background and Issues, by Roger Walke.

Departmental Offices and Department-Wide Programs[29]

Office of Insular Affairs

The Office of Insular Affairs (OIA) provides financial assistance to four insular areas — American Samoa, the Commonwealth of the Northern Mariana Islands (CNMI), Guam, and the U.S. Virgin Islands — as well as three former insular areas — the Federated States of Micronesia (FSM), the Republic of the Marshall Islands (RMI), and the Republic of Palau. OIA staff manage relations between each jurisdiction and the federal government and work to build the fiscal and governmental capacity of units of local government.

Most of OIA's budget is not subject to the annual appropriations process. Specifically, $324.1 million in OIA's FY2008 budget request represented permanent and indefinite funding required by statutes that provide various forms of financial assistance to current and former U.S. territories. In the FY2008 Consolidated Appropriations Act, OIA received $83.1 million in annually appropriated funds. That amount exceeded by $1.6 million (2%) the $81.5 million enacted in FY2007. The $83.1 million is divided into two accounts: Assistance to Territories (AT) and Compact of Free Association (CFA). AT funding provides grants for the operation of the government of American Samoa, infrastructure improvement projects on many of the insular area islands, and specified natural resource initiatives. The CFA account provides federal assistance to the freely associated states pursuant to compact agreements negotiated with the U.S. government. In FY2008, OIA will receive $77.8 million in AT funding (with the rescission), and $5.3 million in CFA appropriations (with the rescission).

In both the AT and CFA accounts, approved funding levels remained largely consistent across the House, Senate committee, and enacted appropriations bills for FY2008. The FY2008 appropriations law designated $70.1 million in AT funding (without the rescission) for technical and maintenance assistance, disaster assistance, brown tree snake control and research, judiciary grants in American Samoa, other grants to individual territories, and other territorial assistance. Of the remaining AT funding, $8.5 million (without the rescission) was designated for OIA salaries and expenses. The law specified conditions for release of AT funding, such as Government Accountability Office (GAO) audits, and specified grants to the Northern Mariana Islands, the Pacific Basin Development Council, and the

Close Up Foundation. OIA funding has been the subject of little congressional debate in recent years.

For additional information on *Insular Affairs,* see its website at [http://www.doi.gov/oia/index.html].

Payments in Lieu of Taxes Program (PILT)

For FY2008, the appropriation for PILT was $228.9 million, a drop of $3.6 million (2%) from the FY2007 level of $232.5 million and 62.5% of the authorized amount. The Administration had requested $190.0 million for PILT, down $42.5 million (18%) from FY2007. The Administration's request would have provided approximately 51.9% of the authorized amount. See table 13.

Table 13. Authorized and Appropriated Levels for Payments in Lieu of Taxes, FY2000-FY2008 ($ in millions)

Fiscal Year	Authorized Amount	Appropriated Amount	% of Authorized Amount
2000	317.6	134.0	42.2
2001	338.6	199.2	58.8
2002	350.8	210.0	59.9
2003	324.1	218.2	67.3
2004	331.3	224.3	67.7
2005	332.0	226.8	68.3
2006	344.4	232.5	67.5
2007	358.3	232.5	64.9
2008 Request	366.2	190.0	51.9
2008 House Passed	366.2	252.7	69.0
2008 Senate Committee	366.2	232.5	63.5
P.L. 110-161	366.2	228.9	62.5

Notes: The FY2008 authorized level, in *italics,* is an estimate. Calculation of the level assumes (1) all revenues from other payment programs are flat over the period; (2) the number of acres eligible for PILT payments is unchanged; (3) all of the counties' populations are unchanged; and (4) no states change their "pass-through" laws. In consequence, only the changes in the Consumer Price Index would influence PILT payments. However, it is likely that at least some of these assumptions would need to be modified, if only marginally. PILT payment levels could become particularly difficult to predict in the future, depending on the enactment of legislation to amend the Secure Rural Schools program. Some versions of this legislation would offer counties the choice of this program's payments *or* PILT payments.

The PILT program compensates local governments for federal land within their jurisdictions which cannot be taxed. Since the beginning of the program in 1976, payments of more than $3.6 billion have been made. The PILT program has been controversial, because in recent years the payment formula, which was indexed for inflation in 1994, has increased authorization levels. However, appropriations have grown less rapidly, and substantially slower than authorized amounts, ranging from 42% to 68% of authorized levels between FY2000 and FY2007.[30] See table 13. County governments claim that the program as a whole does not provide funding comparable to property taxes, and that rural areas in particular need additional PILT funds to provide the kinds of services that counties with more private land are able to provide.

For further information on the *Payments in Lieu of Taxes* program, see the DOI website at [http://www.doi.gov/pilt/].

CRS Report RL31392. PILT (Payments in Lieu of Taxes): Somewhat Simplified, by M. Lynne Corn.

CRS Report RL33822. The Secure Rural Schools and Community Self-Determination Act of 2000: Forest Service Payments to Counties, by Ross. W. Gorte.

Office of Special Trustee for American Indians

The Office of Special Trustee for American Indians (OST), in the Secretary of the Interior's office, was authorized by Title III of the American Indian Trust Fund Management Reform Act of 1994 (25 U.S.C. §§4001, et seq.). The OST generally oversees the reform of Interior Department management of Indian trust assets, establishment of an adequate trust fund management system, and support of department claims settlement activities related to the trust funds. OST also manages Indian funds directly. Indian trust funds formerly were managed by the BIA, but in 1996 the Secretary transferred trust fund management to the OST.

Indian trust funds managed by the OST comprise two sets of funds: (1) tribal funds owned by about 300 tribes in approximately 1,450 accounts, with a total asset value of about $2.9 billion; and (2) individual Indians' funds, known as Individual Indian Money (IIM) accounts, in about 323,000 accounts with a current total asset value of about $400 million.[31] The funds include monies received from claims awards, land or water rights settlements, and other one-time payments, and from income from land-based trust assets (e.g., land, timber, minerals), as well as from investment income.

OST's FY2007 appropriation was $223.3 million. For FY2008, the Consolidated Appropriations Act provided $189.3 million for the OST, a decrease of $33.9 million (15%) from FY2007. The Administration had proposed $196.2 million for FY2008, the House had approved $192.5 million, and the Senate Appropriations Committee had recommended $195.9 million. See table 14. Key issues for the OST are an historical accounting for tribal and IIM accounts, and litigation involving tribal and IIM accounts.

Table 14. Appropriations for the Office of Special Trustee for American Indians, FY2007-FY2008 ($ in thousands)

Office of Special Trustee for American Indians	FY2007 Approp.	FY2008 Request	FY2008 House Passed	FY2008 Senate Comm.	FY2008 Approp.
Federal Trust Programs	189,251	186,158	182,542	185,947	179,487
— Historical Accounting Office	56,384	60,000	56,384	60,000	55,504
Indian Land Consolidation	34,006	10,000	10,000	10,000	9,844
Total Appropriations	223,257	196,158	192,542	195,947	189,331

Historical Accounting

For FY2008, the Administration and the Senate Appropriations Committee supported $60.0 million for historical accounting activities, an increase of 5% over FY2007. The House had approved $56.4 million, the same as FY2007 and $3.6 million (6%) below the Administration's proposal. The FY2008 Consolidated Appropriations Act limited historical accounting to no more than $56.4 million; the rescission reduced this amount to $55.5 million, $0.9 million (2%) less than FY2007. The historical accounting effort seeks to assign correct balances to all tribal and IIM accounts, especially because of litigation. Because of the long historical period to be covered (some accounts date from the 19th century), the large number of IIM accounts, and the large number of missing account documents, an historical accounting based on actual account transactions is expected to be large and time-consuming. In 2003, DOI proposed an extensive, five-year, $335 million project to reconcile IIM accounts. The plan has been revised to reflect ongoing experience and to add additional accounts. The project seeks to reconcile all transactions for certain types of accounts and all land-based transactions of $5,000 and over, but uses a statistical sampling approach to reconcile land-based transactions of less than $5,000. OST continues to follow this plan, subject to court rulings (see "Litigation," below) or congressional actions, and now estimates its completion in FY2011.

Plaintiffs in the *Cobell* litigation (discussed below) consider the statistical sampling technique invalid. Tribal trust fund and accounting suits have been filed for over 300 tribes. Most of the tribal suits were filed at the end of 2006, because the statute of limitations on such claims expired then. OST has been allocating about $40 million of its historical accounting expenditures to IIM accounts and the remainder to tribal accounts. In the past, the House Appropriations Committee has expressed its intent to limit expenditures for historical accounting, asserting it reduces spending on other Indian programs.

Litigation

An IIM trust funds class-action lawsuit (*Cobell* v. *Kempthorne*) was filed in 1996, in the federal district court for the District of Columbia, against the federal government by IIM account holders.[32] Many OST activities are related to the *Cobell* case, including litigation support activities. The most significant issue for appropriations concerns the method for the historical accounting to estimate IIM accounts' proper balances. The DOI estimated its method would cost $335 million over five years and produce a total owed to IIM accounts in the low millions. The plaintiffs' method, based on estimated rates of errors applied to an agreed-upon figure for IIM throughput, was estimated to produce a total owed to IIM accounts of as much as $177 *billion*, depending on the error rate used.

After a lengthy trial, the court, on September 25, 2003, rejected both the plaintiffs' and DOI's historical accounting plans and ordered DOI to account for all trust fund and asset transactions since 1887, without using statistical sampling. DOI estimated that the court's choice for historical accounting would cost $6 billion-$12 billion, and appealed the order. The U.S. Court of Appeals for the District of Columbia temporarily stayed the September 25 order and, on December 10, 2004, overturned much of the order. On February 23, 2005, however, the district court issued an order on historical accounting very similar to its September 2003 order, requiring that an accounting cover all trust fund and asset transactions since 1887 and not use statistical sampling. The DOI, which estimated that compliance with the new order would cost $12-$13 billion,[33] appealed the new order. The Appeals Court on November 15, 2005, vacated the district court's February 2005 order. The district court has not issued another order, and the OST continues its historical accounting under its September 2003 plan. In 2006 the D.C. Circuit assigned a new judge to the *Cobell* case. In October 2007 the judge held hearings on DOI's historical accounting obligations, methodology, and results.

Congress has long been concerned that the current and potential costs of the *Cobell* lawsuit may jeopardize DOI trust reform implementation, reduce spending on other Indian programs, and be difficult to fund. Besides the ongoing expenses of the litigation, possible costs include $12-$13 billion for the court-ordered historical accounting, a *Cobell* settlement that might cost as much as (1) the court-ordered historical accounting, (2) the more than $100 billion that *Cobell* plaintiffs estimate their IIM accounts are owed, or (3) the $27.5 billion that the *Cobell* plaintiffs have proposed as a settlement amount.[34] The addition of tribal trust fund and accounting suits may greatly enlarge the potential costs of a settlement, since tribes' funds are far larger in size than individuals' funds.

Among the funding sources for these large costs discussed in a 2005 House Interior Appropriations Subcommittee hearing were discretionary appropriations and the Treasury Department's "Judgment Fund,"[35] but some senior appropriators consider the Fund insufficient even for a $6-$13 billion dollar settlement.[36] Among other options, Congress may enact another delay to the court-ordered accounting, direct a settlement, or delineate the department's historical accounting obligations (which could limit, or increase, the size of the historical accounting). Settlement bills in the 109th Congress would have established in the Treasury Department's general fund an IIM claim settlement fund with appropriations from the Judgment Fund, but did not specify the dollar size of the fund. The Administration, on March 1, 2007, proposed a comprehensive settlement and a settlement amount of $7 billion, but the proposed settlement would not only cover both IIM and tribal accounting claims but would also settle all trust land mismanagement claims.[37] At a March 29, 2007, hearing before the Senate Indian Affairs Committee, both a Cobell plaintiff and a tribal representative opposed the Administration's proposal, and the Committee chair expressed numerous doubts.[38] No trust fund settlement legislation has been introduced thus far in the 110th Congress. The House Appropriations Committee urged the parties to the litigation, and Congress, to settle trust litigation in its entirety (H.Rept. 110-187, p. 80).

For further information on the *Office of Special Trustee for American Indians*, see its website at [http://www.ost.doi.gov/].

CRS Report RS22343. Indian Trust Fund Litigation: Legislation to Resolve Accounting Claims in Cobell v. Norton, by M. Maureen Murphy.

CRS Report RS21738. The Indian Trust Fund Litigation: An Overview of Cobell v. Norton, by M. Maureen Murphy.

National Indian Gaming Commission

The National Indian Gaming Commission (NIGC) was established by the Indian Gaming Regulatory Act (IGRA) of 1988 (25 U.S.C. §§2701, et seq.) to oversee Indian tribal regulation of tribal bingo and other *Class II* operations, as well as aspects of *Class III* gaming (e.g., casinos and racing).[39] The primary appropriations issue for NIGC is whether its funding is adequate for its regulatory responsibilities.

The NIGC is authorized to receive annual appropriations of $2 million, but its budget authority consists chiefly of annual fees assessed on tribes' Class II and III operations. During FY1999-FY2008, all NIGC activities have been funded from fees, with no direct appropriations. Neither the Administration, the House, nor the Senate Appropriations Committee recommended a direct appropriation for the NIGC for FY2008.

The NIGC in recent years had expressed a need for additional funding because it was experiencing increased demand for its oversight resources, especially audits and field investigations. IGRA formerly capped NIGC fees at $8 million per year, but Congress used appropriations act language to increase the NIGC's fee ceiling to $12 million for FY2004-FY2007. In the Native American Technical Corrections Act of 2006 (P.L. 109-221), Congress amended IGRA to create a formula-based fee ceiling — 0.08% of the gross gaming revenues of all gaming operations subject to regulation under IGRA. This new fee ceiling applied to FY2007 and subsequent fiscal years, superseding the previous dollar limitation for FY2007. The NIGC sets an annual fee rate, which can be less than the ceiling rate.

For FY2007, based on the FY2007 fee rate of .059%, NIGC anticipated fee revenues of $16 million, about a one-third increase from its FY2006 fee revenues of $12 million. NIGC anticipates FY2008 fee revenues of about $18 million.

For further information on the *National Indian Gaming Commission*, see its website at [http://www.nigc.gov].

Chapter 5

TITLE II: ENVIRONMENTAL PROTECTION AGENCY

EPA was established in 1970 to consolidate federal pollution control responsibilities that had been divided among several federal agencies. EPA's responsibilities grew significantly as Congress enacted an increasing number of environmental laws as well as major amendments to these statutes. Among the agency's primary responsibilities are the regulation of air quality, water quality, pesticides, and toxic substances; the management and disposal of solid and hazardous wastes; and the cleanup of environmental contamination. EPA also awards grants to assist state and local governments in controlling pollution.

EPA's funding over time generally has reflected an increase in overall appropriations to fulfill a rising number of statutory responsibilities.[40] Without adjusting for inflation, the agency's appropriation has risen from about $1.0 billion when the agency was established in FY1970 to a high of $8.4 billion in FY2004. Title II of Division F of the FY2008 Consolidated Appropriations Act provided a total of $7.46 billion for EPA. Although the enacted funding level is an increase above the President's request of $7.20 billion, it is less than the $8.09 billion that the House had proposed, the $7.77 billion that the Senate Appropriations Committee had recommended, and the $7.73 billion that Congress had enacted for FY2007.

Congress allocated the FY2008 appropriation of $7.46 billion for EPA among eight statutory accounts that fund the agency, and specified statutory funding levels within these accounts for a relatively small number of selected programs and activities. As in past years, Congress specified funding for most of EPA's programs and activities within the explanatory statement accompanying the FY2008 law,[41] rather than in the statute itself.

Among individual agency programs and activities, there were varying decreases and increases in funding when comparing the FY2008 enacted appropriation to the amounts that the House, Senate Appropriations Committee, and President had supported for FY2008, and Congress had enacted for FY2007. For some activities, funding enacted for FY2008 remained relatively flat, compared to the originally proposed amounts and the prior year appropriation.

Table 15 lists the eight statutory accounts that currently fund EPA.[42] The table specifies the amounts within each of these accounts that Congress enacted for FY2008, and compares these amounts to the initial recommendations of the House and the Senate Appropriations Committee, the President's request, and the amounts that Congress enacted for FY2007. The House had proposed to establish a ninth account in FY2008 to fund a new Commission on Climate Change Adaptation and Mitigation, which is reflected in the following table. The FY2008 law did not include a new account for the House's proposed commission, nor did the law appear to provide funding in any of the agency's other accounts for this purpose. However, the law did provide funding for many other activities related to climate change.

Table 15. Appropriations for the Environmental Protection Agency, FY2007-FY2008 ($ in millions)

Environmental Protection Agency	FY2007 Approp.	FY2008 Request	FY2008 House Passed	FY2008 Senate Comm.	FY2008 Approp.
Science and Technology					
— Base Appropriations	733.4	754.5	783.3	772.5	760.1
— Transfer in from Superfund	30.2	26.1	26.1	26.1	25.7
Science and Technology Total	763.6	780.6	809.4	798.6	785.8
Commission on Climate Change Adaptation and Mitigation[a]	0.0	0.0	50.0	0.0	0.0
Environmental Programs and Management	2,358.4	2,298.2	2,370.6	2,384.1	2,328.0
Office of Inspector General					
— Base Appropriations	37.2	38.0	43.5	40.0	41.1
— Transfer in from Superfund	13.3	7.1	10.0	13.3	11.5

Table 15. (Continued).

Environmental Protection Agency	FY2007 Approp.	FY2008 Request	FY2008 House Passed	FY2008 Senate Comm.	FY2008 Approp.
Office of Inspector General Total	50.5	45.1	53.5	53.3	52.6
Buildings and Facilities	39.6	34.8	34.8	34.8	34.3
Hazardous Substance Superfund Total (before transfers)	1,255.1	1,244.7	1,272.0	1,274.6	1,254.0
— Transfer out to Office of Inspector General	(13.3)	(7.1)	(10.0)	(13.3)	(11.5)
— Transfer out to Science and Technology	(30.2)	(26.1)	(26.1)	(26.1)	(25.7)
Leaking Underground Storage Tank (LUST) Program[b]	72.0	72.5	118.0	72.5	105.8
Oil Spill Response	15.7	17.3	17.3	17.5	17.1
State and Tribal Assistance Grants (STAG)					
— Clean Water SRF	1,083.8	687.6	1,125.0	887.0	689.1
— Drinking Water SRF	837.5	842.2	842.2	842.2	829.0
— Categorical Grants [b]	1,113.1	1,065.0	1,113.8	1,118.4	1,078.3
— Other Grants	179.3	149.7	325.5	334.3	329.8
State and Tribal Assistance Grants Total	3,213.7	2,744.5	3,406.5	3,181.9	2,926.2
Rescission (various EPA accounts)	n/a	[c](5.0)	[c](5.0)	[c](5.0)	[c](5.0)
Total EPA Accounts	7,725.1	7,199.4	8,090.9	7,772.9	7,461.5

Source: Prepared by the Congressional Research Service (CRS) using information in the Explanatory Statement accompanying Division F of the Consolidated Appropriations Act for FY2008 (P.L. 110- 161, H.R. 2764), as published in the *Congressional Record*, December 17, 2007.

[a]. The House recommended a new account to establish a Commission on Climate Change Adaptation and Mitigation. P.L. 110-161 did not fund the House proposal, and neither the Senate Appropriations Committee nor the President proposed funding for such a commission.

[b]. Both the enacted and House-passed amounts for FY2008 include funding within the LUST Program account for specific activities authorized in the Energy Policy Act of 2005 (P.L. 109-58). All other amounts reflect funding for these activities as Categorical Grants within the STAG account. Consequently, these amounts vary partly because of the difference in the accounting of funds for these Energy Policy Act activities.

[c]. P.L. 110-161 included a rescission of $5.0 million in unobligated balances from prior years' appropriations within "various EPA accounts." Although all sources presented this rescission as an offsetting reduction in FY2008, the Administration presented this rescission specifically within the STAG account, as specified in EPA's FY2008 budget justification.

KEY FUNDING ISSUES

Although there were varying levels of interest in the FY2008 debate about the adequacy of funding for individual programs and activities administered by EPA, much of the attention focused on funding for water infrastructure projects, the cleanup of hazardous waste sites under the Superfund and Brownfields programs, scientific research on human health effects upon which pollution control standards are based, and grants to assist state and local governments in administering air quality programs. There also was rising interest in the adequacy of funding and staffing of EPA's Office of Inspector General to audit and evaluate the agency's activities. Funding within EPA and other federal agencies to address climate change has been another area of increasing interest within Congress. Certain EPA regulatory actions also received attention within the funding debate. For example, §432 of Division F of the FY2008 appropriations law prohibited the use of funds to promulgate or implement EPA's proposed rule[43] that would alter Clean Air Act regulations to control hazardous air pollutant emissions from major sources. Selected funding issues that received more prominent attention in the FY2008 appropriations debate are discussed below.

WATER INFRASTRUCTURE

Appropriations for water infrastructure projects are allocated within EPA's State and Tribal Assistance Grants (STAG) account. Most of these funds are devoted to grants that support State Revolving Funds (SRFs). These grant funds provide seed monies for states to issue loans to communities for wastewater and drinking water infrastructure projects. The FY2008 law provided $689.1 million for the Clean Water SRF, slightly more than the President's request of $687.6 million, but far less than the $1.08 billion appropriated for FY2007. The FY2008 enacted appropriation also is much less than the $1.13 billion that the House had proposed, and the $887.0 million that the Senate Appropriations Committee had recommended. The FY2008 law provided another $829.0 million for the Drinking Water SRF. The President had requested $842.2 million, which the House and the Senate Appropriations Committee initially had approved. The FY2008 enacted appropriation for the Drinking Water SRF also was below the prior year appropriation of $837.5 million.

The adequacy of federal funding to assist states in capitalizing their Clean Water SRFs has been an ongoing issue. The Clean Water Act authorized EPA to award grants to help states capitalize these loan funds. Although appropriations for these grants have declined in recent years, Congress still had been providing significantly more funding than the President requested each year. This trend was due to differing views on the extent of the role of the federal government in capitalizing these state loan funds. Departing from this trend, the FY2008 enacted appropriation is closer to the President's request than the higher amounts that Congress had been providing. Over the years, there has been less disagreement between Congress and the Administration in regard to the adequacy of funding for Drinking Water SRF grants. However, some Members continue to assert that more federal funds are needed to help capitalize these loan funds, especially in light of more stringent drinking water standards with which communities must comply.

Although grants to help states capitalize their SRFs represent the bulk of EPA funding for water infrastructure, Congress also has supported these needs through targeted funding for "special project grants" within EPA's STAG account. These grants fund a variety of wastewater, drinking water, and storm water infrastructure projects. They are awarded on a noncompetitive basis to specific communities. Although communities must repay the loan funds that they borrow from the SRFs, special project grants do not require repayment. However, each recipient of these grants must provide 45% of a project's cost in matching funds, unless EPA approves a waiver due to financial hardship.

The FY2008 law provided $132.9 million within the STAG account for 280 special project grants for FY2008, and identified the intended recipients in the explanatory statement accompanying the law.[44] As in past years, the Administration did not request funding for these congressionally designated projects. Total funding for special project grants has declined in the past few years; Congress provided $197.1 million for FY2006. However, Congress did not provide any funding for special project grants in FY2007, as the Revised Continuing Appropriations Resolution for FY2007 (P.L. 110-5) specifically prohibited the funding of these types of grants.

SUPERFUND

The FY2008 law provided $1.22 billion for the Hazardous Substance Superfund account to fund the cleanup of hazardous substances under the

Superfund program. This funding level is the *net* amount available for the program, after a combined transfer of $37.2 million to the S and T account and the Office of the Inspector General account. The President had requested a slightly lower net amount of $1.21 billion for the Superfund account, nearly the same as enacted for FY2007. The House and the Senate Appropriations Committee initially had recommended a greater net amount of $1.24 billion. Funding for the Superfund account has remained relatively close to these amounts over the past decade.

The adequacy of funding for the Superfund program to clean up the nation's most contaminated and threatening sites has been a long-standing issue. The Comprehensive Environmental Response, Compensation, and Liability Act of 1980 (CERCLA) established the Superfund program to fund the cleanup of contamination when responsible parties cannot be found or cannot pay. Some Members of Congress and the Bush Administration continue to assert that a steady level of federal funding is sufficient to maintain a constant pace of cleanup, considering the costs borne by responsible parties that supplement these funds. Other Members, states, environmental organizations, and communities counter that more federal funds are necessary to expedite the pace of cleanup to address human health and environmental risks more quickly, and that the effect of inflation over time has reduced available resources.

The availability of funds within the Superfund account for "physical" cleanup of sites has been a perennial issue, in light of public concerns about health risks from potential exposure to contamination. Although the primary purpose of the Superfund program is to clean up contaminated sites, the program does fund many "indirect" activities that support cleanup, such as enforcement against responsible parties, and research of more effective cleanup methods with funds transferred to the S and T account. In recent years, about 2/3 of annual funding has been devoted to physical cleanup of sites, including both short-term removal actions to address immediate risks and long-term remedial actions intended to provide a more permanent means to prevent exposure.

The FY2008 law provided a total of $827.5 million for activities related to the physical cleanup of sites, an increase above the President's request of $824.5 million and the FY2007 appropriation of $816.9 million. Funding for long-term remedial actions accounted for most of the increase. The FY2008 enacted appropriation is less than the $839.7 million that the House had proposed, and the $843.2 million that the Senate Appropriations Committee had recommended, with the difference again being primarily due to funding for long-term remediation.

In the funding debate, concerns about the sufficiency of cleanup actions to protect human health and the environment also motivated questions about program performance. Staffing and funding of EPA's Office of Inspector General to audit and evaluate the Superfund program were particularly controversial, as discussed in the "Office of Inspector General" section below.

BROWNFIELDS

In addition to the Superfund program, amendments to CERCLA in 2002 established a separate program to clean up contaminated "brownfields." The FY2008 appropriations law provided a combined total of $165.8 million for EPA's Brownfields Program. The House initially had proposed a higher amount of $172.9 million. The Senate Appropriations Committee had recommended $162.5 million, closer to the President's request of $162.2 million and the FY2007 appropriation of $163.0 million. Total funding for the Brownfields Program consists of three amounts. The STAG account funds Brownfields "infrastructure" grants to assist communities with cleanup at individual sites, and Brownfields "categorical" grants to assist states with their own Brownfields programs. The Environmental Programs and Management account funds the administrative expenses of the Brownfields Program.

Typically, brownfields are abandoned, idled, or underutilized commercial and industrial properties with levels of contamination less hazardous than a Superfund site, but that still warrant cleanup before the land can be safe for reuse. The desire to redevelop these properties for economic benefit has generated interest in the adequacy of funding for brownfields cleanup grants to states and local areas. In response to these needs, the FY2008 enacted appropriation included an increase for Brownfields infrastructure grants to assist communities with the cleanup of individual sites, but not as much as the House initially had approved. The enacted amounts for Brownfields categorical grants and administrative expenses of the program are roughly similar to the recommendations of the House, the Senate Appropriations Committee, the President, and the FY2007 appropriation.

Office of Inspector General (OIG)

The Office of Inspector General (OIG) is an independent office within EPA that conducts and supervises audits, evaluations, inspections, and investigations of the agency's programs and operations. The OIG also performs audits and evaluations specifically requested by Congress. The office is funded by a "base" appropriation and a transfer of appropriations from the Superfund account. Historically, Congress has transferred these funds to the OIG because a significant portion of its funding and staffing has been devoted to oversight of EPA's cleanup efforts under the Superfund program. Including the transfer from Superfund, the FY2008 law provided $52.6 million for the OIG, an increase above the President's request of $45.1 million and the FY2007 appropriation of $50.5 million. The House had proposed $53.5 million for FY2008, and the Senate Appropriations Committee had recommended $53.3 million.

In the funding debate, some Members had expressed concern that the President's request would not have been sufficient to support adequate staffing to audit and evaluate Superfund cleanup activities. The explanatory statement accompanying the FY2008 law indicated that the increase in enacted funding above the request and the FY2007 appropriation was intended to ensure consistent staffing levels within the OIG, and was not to be used for buyouts associated with reductions in staff. EPA had reported that the President's proposed decrease in funding for the OIG would have resulted in a reduction of 30 workyears (full time equivalent employees or FTEs), and a reassignment of 20 FTEs from the oversight of Superfund cleanups to oversight of a broader array of agency activities.

Scientific Research

Most of EPA's scientific research activities are funded within the Science and Technology (S and T) account, including the agency's laboratories and research grants. Similar to the OIG account, the S and T account is funded by a base appropriation and a transfer from Superfund. These transferred funds are dedicated to research of more effective methods to clean up contaminated sites. Including the transfer from the Superfund account, the FY2008 law provided $785.8 million for the S and T account, an increase above the President's request of $780.6 million and the FY2007 appropriation of $763.6 million. The House had proposed $809.4 million for this account in FY2008, and the Senate Appropriations Committee had recommended $798.6 million.

Most of the S and T account funds "actual" research activities, but the operational and administrative expenses of agency research facilities, such as rent, utilities, and security, are also funded within this account. The increase above FY2007 was mostly due to a continued shift in funds from the Environmental Programs and Management account to pay these operational and administrative expenses. Consequently, funding enacted for FY2008 for many of EPA's research areas decreased, or remained relatively flat, relative to FY2007. However, funding for certain areas rose above the President's request for FY2008 and the prior year appropriation, such as Climate Protection and Global Change research areas, but not to the level that the House or the Senate Appropriations Committee had proposed for FY2008 in some cases.

The funding debate for FY2008 took place within the context of a larger discussion about the adequacy of federal funding for many "core" scientific research activities administered by multiple federal agencies, including EPA. Some Members of Congress, scientists, and environmental organizations have expressed concern about the downward trend in federal resources for scientific research over time. The debate continues to center around the question of whether the regulatory actions of federal agencies are based on "sound science," and how scientific research is applied in developing federal policy.

State and Local Air Quality Management Grants

The FY2008 law provided $216.8 million for state and local air quality management categorical grants within EPA's STAG account, an increase above the President's request of $185.2 million and the FY2007 appropriation of $199.8 million. Some Members and state and local air pollution control officials have continued to express that even greater funds are needed for these grants, as a result of increasing Clean Air Act responsibilities imposed upon state and local governments to regulate air pollution. The FY2008 enacted appropriation for these grants was less than the $220.2 million that the House had proposed and the $220.3 million that the Senate Appropriations Committee had recommended.

According to EPA, the President's requested decrease for state and local air quality management grants was primarily because of the agency's use of different authorities in the Clean Air Act to administer these grants. EPA originally proposed this change in authorities in its FY2007 budget justification. These different grant authorities require matching funds from recipients, rather than the federal government bearing the full cost. EPA based this proposed shift in authorities on its assertion that the monitoring network for particulate matter is beyond the demonstration phase, and that the network should now be considered an operational system in the implementation phase. Authorities for demonstration grants do not require matching funds, but those for implementation do require a match, thereby reducing the federal role in funding these activities.

In its initial report on the FY2008 Interior appropriations bill, the Senate Appropriations Committee had "strongly" disagreed with the President's proposed shift in grant authorities to require matching funds of recipients (S.Rept. 110-91, p. 69). The FY2008 law and the explanatory statement accompanying the law did not explicitly address this issue. However, the statement did specify that House or Senate report language that was not changed by the explanatory statement "should be treated as approved when administering the appropriations" (Explanatory Statement, H16122). Presumably, EPA would be subject to the language in the original Senate report, expressing the intention of the committee not to require matching funds for these air quality grants.

PROPOSED COMMISSION ON CLIMATE CHANGE

The FY2008 law did not include a new account, or funding in any other existing account, to establish a new Commission on Climate Change Adaptation and Mitigation. The House had proposed $50.0 million for a new account for this purpose. The commission would have been temporary and would have served for two years. Neither the Senate Appropriations Committee, nor the President, recommended funding for such a commission.

Of the $50.0 million that the House had proposed, $5.0 million was to have been used to establish and operate the commission, analyze scientific questions related to climate change adaptation and mitigation, and recommend research priorities to better understand climate change. The remaining $45.0 million was to have been distributed to various federal agencies to conduct this research, based on the commission's recommended priorities. The agencies that would have received this funding would not have been limited to those funded in the Interior appropriations bill. The commission would have been made up of individuals inside and outside of government, and the President of the National Academy of Sciences would have served as the chairman.

For further information on the Environmental Protection Agency's budget and activities, see its websites [http://www.epa.gov] and [http://epa.gov/ocfo/budget/].

Chapter 6

TITLE III: RELATED AGENCIES

DEPARTMENT OF AGRICULTURE: FOREST SERVICE

For the Forest Service (FS), the FY2008 Consolidated Appropriations Act contained $4.67 billion, including $222.0 million in emergency appropriations for wildfire suppression in Title V. An additional $329.0 million in emergency wildfire funds was provided in an earlier law, P.L. 110-116, for a total FS appropriation of $5.0 billion for FY2008. This total was higher than enacted for FY2007 and supported by the President, House, and Senate Appropriations Committee for FY2008, primarily due to the emergency fire money. In general, Congress rejected the decreases that the Administration had proposed across a range of line items and programs, as an offset to recent increases for fire suppression. The Senate Appropriations Committee expressed that "[f]orcing the Forest Service to absorb rapid increases in firefighting costs within discretionary funds shortchanges vital fire preparedness and natural resource programs and undermines the agency's multiple-use mission" (S.Rept. 110-91, p. 79).

As shown in figure 1, FS appropriations are provided in several major accounts: Forest and Rangeland Research (FS Research); State and Private Forestry; National Forest System; Wildland Fire Management; Capital Improvement and Maintenance (Capital); Land Acquisition; and Other programs. For FY2008, about half of the total FS appropriation — $2.49 billion of the $5.0 billion — was provided for wildland fire management. The Senate Appropriations Committee was "disturbed that the proportion of Forest Service budget that is devoted to fire activities is growing rapidly while the overall budget declines" (S.Rept. 110-91, p. 79). The committee noted that in 2000 fire programs accounted for 21% of the FS budget, whereas in the FY2008 budget request they represented 45%.

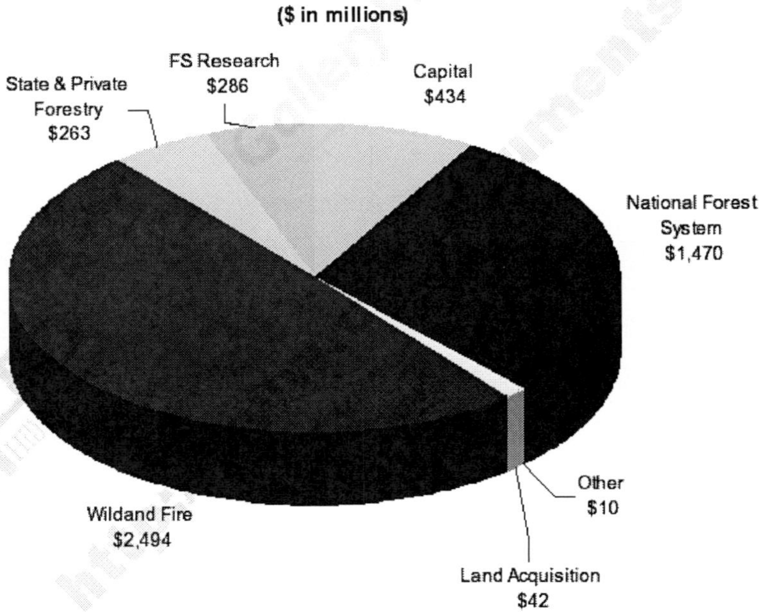

Figure 1. FS FY2008 Appropriation ($ in millions).

Major FS Issues in Appropriations

Significant FS issues have been raised during consideration of the annual Interior appropriations bills. In the FS budget proposals for FY2007 and FY2008, the President proposed selling about 300,000 acres of national forest lands. In the FY2007 request, the proceeds would have paid for a five-year extension of FS payments under the Secure Rural Schools and Community Self-Determination Act of 2000 (P.L. 106-393). In the FY2008 request, the proceeds were proposed to be split, with half for a four-year phase-out of payments under P.L. 106-393 and the other half for habitat improvement and land acquisition. Legislation would be needed to authorize the proposed land sale, but such legislation has not been enacted. The House Appropriations Committee "strongly encourage[d] the Administration to permanently abandon this notion" of "selling off national forest system lands to generate funds for rural schools" (H.Rept. 110-187, p. 120). A one-year extension of payments under P.L. 106-393 was included in P.L. 110-28. On the House floor, an amendment was offered to the FY2008 Interior appropriations bill to add $425.0 million for another year's payments under the program, but the amendment was not in order. Reauthorization of Secure Rural Schools — without land sales — is still being debated.

The FY2008 law did not include House-passed language that would have limited funds for timber harvesting in the Tongass (AK) National Forest. The House had agreed to an amendment to prohibit funds to plan, design, study, or build forest development roads in the Tongass for timber harvesting by private entities or individuals (§503). Proponents of the amendment contended that timber harvests in the Tongass are a net loss to the Treasury and damaging to the environment; opponents asserted that federal timber is critical to the economy of southeast Alaska. A similar amendment had passed the House in the FY2006 appropriations bill but was removed in the conference agreement. In the FY2007 bill, the amendment was disallowed on a point of order.

Wildland Fire Management

Fire funding and fire protection programs continue to be controversial. Ongoing discussions include questions about the high cost of fire suppression efforts; locations for various fire protection treatments; and whether, and to what extent, environmental analysis, public involvement, and challenges to decisions hinder fuel reduction and post-fire rehabilitation activities.

The FS and BLM wildfire line items include funds for fire suppression (fighting fires), preparedness (equipment, training, baseline personnel, prevention, and detection), and other operations (rehabilitation, fuel reduction, research, and state and private assistance). The FY2008 appropriations law contained $3.05 billion for these line items. Another $0.5 billion in emergency funds for wildfires was included in P.L. 110-116, for an FY2008 total of $3.55 billion for FS and BLM wildfire funding combined. As shown in Table 16, this would be the highest level in at least five years. About 30% of the FY2008 total ($1.06 billion) was provided to the BLM; this funding is discussed in the "Bureau of Land Management" section in this book. About 70% of the FY2008 total ($2.49 billion) was provided to the FS.

Of the FS fire funds, the largest portion was for fire suppression — $1,067.6 million. This would fund the ten-year average of fire suppression and provide additional funds ($222.0 million in Title V) if needed for an extreme fire season (Explanatory Statement, H16139). The House Appropriations Committee expressed continued concern with the high costs of large fires, and provided direction to the FS and DOI on examining, reducing, and reporting on the costs of large fire incidences.

For FS preparedness, the FY2008 law contained $665.8 million, essentially level with FY2007 but a large increase over the Administration's request for FY2008. Both the House and the Senate Appropriations Committees rejected the

Administration's cut as "irresponsible." The House Committee asserted that it would "impair the ability of the Forest Service and its partners to launch successful initial attacks, thereby making more destructive and expensive fires not just possible, but inevitable." (H.Rept 110-187, p. 137; S.Rept. 110-91 p. 79). Both Committees expressed dissatisfaction that the FS and DOI have not deployed the Fire Program Analysis system as an "urgently needed fire preparedness planning tool," and provided direction for doing so (Explanatory Statement, p. H16138).

For other fire programs, the FY2008 law provided $432.0 million for the FS. The Administration had sought to reduce funding for other operations through cuts for hazardous fuels and state fire assistance and eliminating funds for post-fire site rehabilitation. The FY2008 law did not reflect these proposals. Most of the FY2008 appropriation for other programs was for hazardous fuels reduction — $310.1 million, or 72%. The Appropriations Committees provided direction regarding these funds, such as their allocation based on a model that prioritizes fuels treatments in the wildland-urban interface and gives greater weight to areas with high fuel loads, population, and values at risk.

P.L. 110-116 provided $329.0 million in emergency fire funds for the FS for FY2008. The appropriation was for several purposes: $110.0 million for emergency wildfire suppression; $100.0 million for repayment of accounts from which funds were borrowed during FY2007 for wildfire suppression; $80.0 million for hazardous fuels reduction and hazard mitigation activities; $25.0 million for rehabilitation and restoration of lands; and $14.0 million for reconstruction/construction of facilities.

Table 16. Appropriations for FS and BLM Wildland Fire Management, FY2004-FY2008 ($ in millions)

National Fire Plan	FY2004 Approp.	FY2005 Approp.	FY2006 Approp.	FY2007 Approp.	FY2008 Request	FY2008 House Passed	FY2008 Senate Comm.	FY2008 Approp.
Forest Service								
— Fire suppression[a]	1,296.0	1,044.4	790.2	1,111.5	911.0	859.0	859.0	1,067.6
— Preparedness	671.6	676.5	660.7	665.4	568.8	675.4	676.4	665.8
— Other operations[b]	379.0	407.7	395.2	416.7	388.8	440.2	447.1	432.0
Emergency Approps. (P.L. 110-116)	—	—	—	—	—	—	—	329.0
Subtotal, FS	2,346.6	2,128.6	1,846.1	2,193.6	1,868.6	1,974.6	1,982.5	2,494.5
BLM								
— Fire suppression[a]	391.3	317.0	330.7	344.2	294.4	294.4	294.4	367.8
— Preparedness[c]	254.2	258.9	268.8	274.9	268.3	274.9	286.0	276.5
— Other Operations	238.1	255.3	255.7	234.3	239.1	237.4	249.1	241.8
— Emergency Approps. (P.L. 110-116)	—	—	—	—	—	—	—	171.0
Subtotal, BLM	883.6	831.3	855.3	853.4	801.8	806.6	829.5	1,057.1
FS and BLM								
— Fire suppression[a]	1,687.3	1,361.4	1,120.9	1,455.7	1,205.4	1,153.4	1,153.4	1,435.4
— Preparedness	925.8	935.4	929.5	940.3	837.1	950.2	962.4	942.3
— Other Operations	617.1	663.0	650.9	651.0	627.9	677.6	696.2	673.8
— Emergency Approps. (P.L. 110-116)	—	—	—	—	—	—	—	500.0
Total Funding	3,230.2	2,959.8	2,701.3	3,047.0	2,670.4	2,781.3	2,812.0	3,551.5

Notes: Includes funding only from BLM and FS Wildland Fire Management accounts.

This table differs from the detailed tables in CRS Report RL33990, *Wildfire Funding*, by Ross W. Gorte, because that report rearranges data to distinguish funding for protecting federal lands, assisting in nonfederal land protection, and fire research and other activities.

a. Includes emergency supplemental and contingent appropriations for FY2004 — FY2008.

b. Excludes fire assistance funding under the State and Private Forestry line item.

c. Fire research and fuel reduction funds are included under Other Operations.

State and Private Forestry

State and Private Forestry (S and PF) programs provide financial and technical assistance to states and to private forest owners. For FY2008, the law contained \$262.7 million for S and PF, a decrease of \$17.3 million (6%) from FY2007 but an increase of \$60.2 million (30%) over the Administration's FY2008 request. See table 17. The request had included relatively large cuts for cooperative lands forest health management, forest stewardship, forest legacy, and urban and community forestry. The FY2008 law reduced appropriations for all four programs from FY2007, but not to the degree sought by the Administration.

Forest health management programs provide insect and disease control on federal and cooperative (nonfederal) lands. The FY2008 appropriation of \$44.5 million for cooperative lands was a 5% reduction from FY2007, but an increase of 17% over the Administration's request. The other three programs are funded under Cooperative Forestry. For the forest stewardship program, which assists private landowners, the FY2008 appropriation was \$29.5 million — 30% lower than FY2007 but 48% higher than the request. The forest legacy program assists states and private landowners through purchase of title or easements for lands threatened with conversion to nonforest uses, such as for residences. The FY2008 appropriation of \$52.2 million was 8% lower than FY2007, but 78% higher than the request. Another \$7.5 million in prior year funds was provided for FY2008, making \$59.7 million in available funding. The urban and community forestry programs provides financial and technical assistance to localities. The FY2008 appropriation of \$27.7 million was a reduction of 8% from FY2007 but an increase of 59% over the request.

Table 17. Appropriations for FS State and Private Forestry, FY2005-FY2008 ($ in millions)

State and Private Forestry	FY2005 Approp.	FY2006 Approp.	FY2007 Approp.	FY2008 Request	FY2008 House Passed	FY2008 Senate Comm.	FY2008 Approp.
Forest Health Management	101.9	100.1	101.1	91.1	101.1	102.2	98.7
— Federal Lands	54.2	53.2	54.0	53.0	54.0	55.0	54.1
— Cooperative Lands	47.6	46.9	47.1	38.1	47.1	47.2	44.5
Cooperative Fire Assistance	38.8	38.8	38.8	42.1	42.1	39.0	38.5
— State Assistance	32.9	32.9	32.9	33.1	33.1	33.1	32.6
— Volunteer Asst.	5.9	5.9	5.9	9.0	9.0	5.9	5.9
Cooperative Forestry	145.4	133.2	133.2	66.7	129.4	124.3	118.1
— Forest Stewardship	32.3	34.1	41.9	20.0	36.9	34.3	29.5
— Forest Legacy[a]	57.1	56.5	56.5	29.3	56.3	48.1	52.2
— Urban and Comm. Forestry	32.0	28.4	30.1	17.4	31.1	30.8	27.7
— Economic Action Prog.	19.0	9.5	0.0	0.0	0.0	6.5	4.2
— Forest Res. Info. and Anal.	5.0	4.6	4.6	0.0	5.0	4.6	4.5
International Programs	6.4	6.9	6.9	2.5	8.0	7.0	7.4
Emergency Appropriations	49.1	30.0	0.0	0.0	0.0	0.0	0.0
Total State and Private Forestry	341.6	309.0	280.0	202.5	280.6	272.5	262.7

a. For FY2008, the House and the Senate Appropriations Committee both provided an additional $6.5 million to be available from prior year balances, while the FY2008 law provided an additional $7.5 million in prior year balances.

Other Programs

For the *National Forest System*, the FY2008 law provided nearly level funding — $1.47 billion. Each of the major activities received level or increased funding relative to FY2007, except that there was a 15% reduction for land management planning (to $48.8 million). The largest increase was for law enforcement — from $115.0 million in FY2007 to $131.9 million in FY2008. The President had sought a decrease for the National Forest System to $1.34 billion (8%), with the decrease spread among many programs. The President had sought an increase only for law enforcement (to $123.8 million).

For *Capital Improvement and Maintenance* (infrastructure), the FY2008 law provided slightly reduced appropriations — $434.4 million. However, it contained an additional $40.0 million, comprised of transfers of $25.0 million from the purchaser elect road fund and $15.0 million from the road and trails fund. Similar transfers had been supported by the House. The FY2008 appropriation included $48.3 million for deferred maintenance, to reduce the agency's backlog (estimated at $5.6 billion). This was a large increase over the $9.1 million appropriated for FY2007 and supported by the Administration and the Senate committee for FY2008. The deferred maintenance appropriation contained $39.4 million for "legacy road remediation," to decommission roads, repair and maintain roads and trails, remove fish passage barriers, and protect community water resources (Explanatory Statement, H16138). The House had approved a larger amount for legacy road remediation.

For FY2008, the law also provided level funding for *Land Acquisition* — $41.8 million. Funds were provided for 25 specific acquisitions in 20 states, with amounts ranging from less than $0.2 million to approximately $4.5 million. The Administration had sought to cut the appropriation to $15.7 million.

For information on the *Department of Agriculture,* see its website at [http://www.usda.gov/wps/portal/usdahome].

For further information on the *U.S. Forest Service*, see its website at [http://www.fs.fed.us/].

CRS Report RL33792. Federal Lands Managed by the Bureau of Land Management (BLM) and the Forest Service: Issues for the 110th Congress, by Ross W. Gorte, Carol Hardy Vincent, and Marc Humphries.

CRS Report RL30755. *Forest Fire/Wildfire Protection*, by Ross W. Gorte.

CRS Report RL30647. *National Forest System Roadless Areas Initiative,* by Pamela Baldwin and Ross W. Gorte.

CRS Report RL33990. *Wildfire Funding*, by Ross W. Gorte.

DEPARTMENT OF HEALTH AND HUMAN SERVICES: INDIAN HEALTH SERVICE

The Indian Health Service (IHS) in the Department of Health and Human Services (HHS) is responsible for providing comprehensive medical and environmental health services for approximately 1.9 million American Indians and Alaska Natives (AI/AN) who belong to 561 federally recognized tribes located in 35 states. Health care is provided through a system of federal, tribal, and urban Indian-operated programs and facilities. IHS provides direct health care services through 33 hospitals, 52 health centers, 2 school health centers, 38 health stations, and 5 residential treatment centers. Tribes and tribal groups, through IHS contracts and compacts, operate another 15 hospitals, 220 health centers, 9 school health centers, 116 health stations, 166 Alaska Native village clinics, and 28 residential treatment centers. IHS, tribes, and tribal groups also operate 11 regional youth substance abuse treatment centers and 2,252 units of residential quarters for staff working in the clinics.

The FY2008 appropriations law contained \$3.35 billion for the IHS, an increase of \$166.0 million (5%) over FY2007 (\$3.18 billion). The Administration had proposed \$3.27 billion for FY2008, the House had approved \$3.38 billion, and the Senate Appropriations Committee had recommended \$3.37 billion. IHS also receives funding through reimbursements and a special Indian diabetes program (see "Health Services" below). The sum of direct appropriations, reimbursements, and diabetes is IHS's "program level" total. See table 18.

IHS funding is separated into two budget categories: Health Services, and Facilities. Of total IHS appropriations enacted for FY2008, 89% will be used for Health Services and 11% for the Facilities program. The most significant issues in the FY2008 IHS budget concern the urban Indian health program, in Health Services, and the health care facilities construction program in Facilities.

Table 18. Appropriations for the Indian Health Service, FY2007-FY2008 ($ millions)

Indian Health Service	FY2007 Approp.	FY2008 Request	FY2008 House Passed	FY2008 Senate Comm.	FY2008 Approp.
Indian Health Services					
Clinical Services					
— Hospital and Health Clinics	1,442.5	1,493.5	1,493.5	1,503.8	1,470.2
— Dental Health	126.9	135.8	135.8	135.8	133.6
— Mental Health	61.7	64.5	64.5	67.0	63.5
— Alcohol and Substance Abuse	150.5	162.0	162.0	164.5	159.5
— Contract Health Care	517.3	569.5	579.5	579.5	579.3
—— Catastrophic Health Emergency Fund	17.7	18.0	18.0	28.0	26.6
— Methamphetamine treatment and prevention	N/A	0	15.0	0.0	13.8
— Indian Health Care Improvement Fund	N/A	0	25.0	0.0	13.8
Subtotal, Clinical Services	2,298.8	2,425.3	2,475.3	2,450.6	2,433.8
Preventive Health Services					
— Public Health Nursing	53.0	56.8	56.8	56.8	55.9
— Health Education	14.5	15.2	15.2	15.2	15.0
— Community Health Representatives	55.7	55.8	55.8	55.8	54.9
— Immunization (Alaska)	1.7	1.8	1.8	1.8	1.7
Subtotal, Preventive Health Services	124.9	129.6	129.6	129.6	127.6
Other Services					
— Urban Health Projects	34.0	0	34.0	35.1	34.5
— Indian Health Professions	31.7	31.9	36.9	31.9	36.3
— Tribal Management	2.5	2.5	2.5	2.5	2.5
— Direct Operations	63.8	64.6	64.6	64.6	63.6
— Self-Governance	5.8	5.9	5.9	5.9	5.8
— Contract Support Costs	264.7	271.6	274.6	271.6	267.4
Subtotal, Other Services	402.5	376.6	418.6	411.7	410.2
Subtotal, Indian Health Services	2,826.2	2,931.5	3,023.5	2,991.9	2,971.5
Indian Health Facilities					
— Maintenance and Improvement	52.7	51.9	52.7	53.7	52.9
— Sanitation Facilities Construction	94.0	88.5	94.0	95.7	94.3
— Health Care Facilities Construction	24.3	12.7	20.3	33.0	36.6

Table 18. (Continued).

Indian Health Service	FY2007 Approp.	FY2008 Request	FY2008 House Passed	FY2008 Senate Comm.	FY2008 Approp.
— Facilities and Environmental Health Support	161.3	164.8	172.3	170.6	169.6
— Equipment	21.6	21.3	21.6	22.4	21.3
Subtotal, Indian Health Facilities	353.9	339.2	360.9	375.5	374.6
Total Appropriations	3,180.1	3,270.7	3,384.4	3,367.4	3,346.2
Medicare/Medicaid Reimbursements and Other Collections	648.2	700.3	700.3	700.3	700.3
Special Diabetes Program for Indians[a]	150.0	150.0	150.0	150.0	150.0
Total Program Level	3,978.4	4,121.0	4,234.7	4,217.7	4,196.5

Note: N/A = Not available.

a. The Special Diabetes Program for Indians has a direct appropriation of $150 million for each of fiscal years FY2004 through FY2008 (P.L. 107-360). Funded through the General Treasury, this program cost is not a part of IHS appropriations.

Health Services

IHS Health Services are funded not only through congressional appropriations, but also from money reimbursed from private health insurance and federal programs such as Medicare, Medicaid, and the State Children's Health Insurance Program (SCHIP). Estimated total reimbursements are expected to be $700.3 million in FY2008. Another $150.0 million per year is expended through IHS for the Special Diabetes Program for Indians under a separate appropriation that expires after FY2008.

The IHS Health Services budget has three subcategories: clinical services, preventive health services, and other services.

Clinical Services

The clinical services budget includes most of IHS Health Services funding. The FY2008 appropriations law contained $2.43 billion for clinical services, an increase of $135.0 million (6%) over FY2007 ($2.30 billion) and of $8.4 million (<1%) over the Administration's request for FY2008. The House had approved $2.48 billion, and the Senate committee had recommended $2.45 billion.

Clinical services include primary care at IHS- and tribally run hospitals and clinics. For *hospital and health clinic programs*, which make up 60% of the FY2008 clinical services budget, the FY2008 appropriation was $1.47 billion. This was an increase of $27.8 million (2%) over the FY2007 level of $1.44 billion but a decrease of $23.3 million (2%) from the Administration's request. The Administration and the House had both supported $1.49 billion, while the Senate committee had recommended $1.50 billion.

Contract health care is a significant clinical service that funds the purchase of health services from local and community health care providers when IHS cannot provide medical care and specific services through its own system. It is especially important in IHS regions that have fewer direct-care facilities or no inpatient facilities. The FY2008 law appropriated $579.3 million for contract health care, including $26.6 million for the Catastrophic Health Emergency Fund (CHEF). This was a $62.0 million (12%) increase over the FY2007 appropriation ($517.3 million) and $9.8 million (2%) higher than the level requested by the Administration for FY2008 ($569.5 million). The House and the Senate Appropriations Committee had both approved $579.5 million, nearly the level that was appropriated. However, the Senate committee had recommended increasing CHEF to $28.0 million, an increase of 58% over the FY2007 level of $17.7 million. Both the Administration and House had supported relatively level funding for CHEF — $18.0 million. CHEF is used to pay contract health care costs in critical, high-cost cases (above $25,000), such as disaster victims or catastrophic illnesses.

For *other programs* within clinical services, the FY2008 appropriations law contained $133.6 million for dental programs, $63.5 million for mental health, and $159.5 million for alcohol and substance abuse. The law provided a separate $13.8 million for methamphetamine treatment and prevention and authorized its distribution to areas with greatest need. It also provided $13.8 million for the Indian Health Care Improvement Fund (IHCIF), and the explanatory statement directed that it be allocated first to units with the greatest level of health care funding needs so as to bring their funding up to 40% of the funding needed (as measured by the formula). The IHCIF is authorized to be allocated among IHS service units to reduce health status and resources deficiencies and shortfalls; it is allocated according to a formula that measures the percentage of health care funding needs met in each operating unit. The Administration had proposed that dental programs receive $135.8 million, mental health programs $64.5 million, and alcohol and substance abuse programs $162.0 million. The House had approved these proposals, but separately added $15.0 million for methamphetamine treatment and prevention and $25.0 million for IHCIF. The Senate committee had recommended the same amount as the House for dental health but disagreed with the House on other programs. The Committee had recommended adding $2.5 million for methamphetamine programs to the Administration/House amount for alcohol and substance abuse programs (instead of a separate appropriation), adding $2.5 million for suicide prevention to the Administration/House amount for mental health programs, and no funding for IHCIF.

Preventive Health Services

For preventive health services, the FY2008 appropriations law contained $127.6 million, a $2.6 million (2%) increase over FY2007 ($124.9 million). Included were $55.9 million for public health nursing, $15.0 million for health education in schools and communities, $1.7 million for immunizations in Alaska, and $54.9 million for the tribally administered community health representatives program, which supports tribal community members who work to prevent illness and disease in their communities. The Administration, House, and Senate Appropriations Committee had supported $129.6 million for preventive health services, a 4% increase over FY2007.

Other Health Services

The FY2008 appropriations law contained $410.2 million for other health services for FY2008. This was an increase of $7.7 million (2%) over the FY2007 level of $402.5 million and of $33.6 million (9%) over the President's request of $376.6 million. The House had approved $418.6 million for these services, and the Senate committee had recommended $411.7 million.

The FY2008 law appropriated $267.4 million for contract support costs (CSC), the largest item in this category. Contract support costs are provided to tribes to help pay the costs of administering IHS-funded programs under self-determination contracts or self-governance compacts authorized by the Indian Self-Determination and Education Assistance Act (P.L. 93-638, as amended). CSC pays for costs that tribes incur for such items as financial management, accounting, training, and program start-up. The Administration and the Senate Appropriations Committee had supported a higher funding level ($271.6 million) as had the House ($274.6 million.)

Besides urban Indian health programs (discussed below), other health services include Indian health professions scholarships and other support, for which the FY2008 law appropriated $36.3 million; tribal management grants ($2.5 million); direct IHS operation of facilities ($63.6 million); and self-governance technical assistance ($5.8 million).

Urban Indian Health Program

The FY2008 appropriations law contained $34.5 million for the urban Indian health program, a 2% increase over the FY2007 level of $34.0 million. The Administration had proposed no FY2008 funding for the program, but the House and Senate Appropriations Committee had disagreed; they approved $34.0 million and $35.1 million respectively.

The 28-year-old program helps fund preventive and primary health services for eligible urban Indians through contracts and grants with 34 urban Indian organizations at 41 urban sites. The specific services vary from site to site, and may include direct clinical care, alcohol and substance abuse care, referrals, and health information. The Administration contends that IHS must target funding and services towards Indians on or near reservations, to serve those who do not have access to health care other than IHS, and that urban Indians can be served through other federal and local health programs, such as HHS's Health Centers program. Opponents assert that the Administration has not provided evidence that alternative programs can replace the urban Indian health program and that it has not studied the impact of the loss of IHS funding on health care for urban Indians who annually receive services through this program. The House Appropriations Committee made similar assertions and added that the urban Indian health program "provides vital, culturally sensitive health care" (H.Rept. 110-187, p. 146).

Facilities

The IHS's Facilities category includes money for the equipment, construction, maintenance, and improvement of both health-care and sanitation facilities, as well as environmental health support programs. The FY2008 appropriations law contained $374.6 million for FY2008, an increase of $20.7 million (6%) over the FY2007 level of $353.9 million and of $35.5 million (10%) over the Administration's request of $339.2 million. The House had approved $360.9 million, while the Senate Appropriations Committee had recommended $375.5 million. Included in the facilities total for FY2008 was $52.9 million for maintenance and improvement, $94.3 million for sanitation facilities construction, $21.3 million for equipment, $169.6 million for facilities and environmental health support, and $36.6 million for health care facilities construction (discussed below). See table 18.

Health Care Facilities Construction

The $36.6 million in the FY2008 appropriations law for health facilities construction was 51% more than FY2007 and 189% more than the Administration's proposal. The act's explanatory statement specified amounts (without the rescission) for construction of hospitals and clinics ($32.7 million), small ambulatory facilities ($2.5 million), and dental units ($2.0 million). Instead of recommending specific projects (as the House and Senate committees had done earlier), the explanatory statement expressed the expectation that the IHS would allocate funding to the highest-priority projects on which construction had begun but for which additional funding was needed to keep the project on schedule.

The FY2007 level for health care facilities construction had been a 36% reduction from the FY2006 level of $37.8 million, which itself had been a 57% reduction from the FY2005 level of $88.6 million. The Administration had proposed $12.7 million for construction of new health care facilities in FY2008, a 48% reduction from the FY2007 level of $24.3 million. The Administration had asserted that its cut was part of an HHS-wide emphasis on maintenance of existing facilities, and that it helped fund the increasing costs of health care services and the staffing of several recently completed facilities. Opponents had contended that the IHS has reported a $1.5 billion backlog in unmet health-facility needs and that the need was too great for a reduction in new construction. The House approved $20.3 million for FY2008, while the Senate committee recommended $33.0 million.

For further information on the Indian Health Service, see its website at [http://www.ihs.gov/].

CRS Report RL33022. Indian Health Service: Health Care Delivery, Status, Funding, and Legislative Issues, by Roger Walke.

OFFICE OF NAVAJO AND HOPI INDIAN RELOCATION

The Office of Navajo and Hopi Indian Relocation (ONHIR) and its predecessor were created pursuant to a 1974 act (P.L. 93-531, as amended) to resolve a lengthy dispute between the Hopi and Navajo tribes involving lands originally set aside by the federal government for a reservation in 1882. Pursuant to the 1974 act, the lands were partitioned between the two tribes. Members of one tribe living on land partitioned to the other tribe were to be relocated and provided new homes, and bonuses, at federal expense. Relocation is to be voluntary.

ONHIR's chief activities consist of land acquisition, housing acquisition or construction, infrastructure construction, and post-move support, all for families being relocated, as well as certification of families' eligibility for relocation benefits. The FY2008 appropriations law contained $8.9 million for ONHIR, a 4% increase over FY2007 ($8.5 million). The Administration, House, and Senate Appropriations Committee had supported $9.0 million.

Navajo-Hopi relocation began in 1977 and is now nearing completion. ONHIR has a backlog of relocatees who are approved for replacement homes but have not yet received them. Most families subject to relocation were Navajo. Originally, an estimated 3,600 eligible Navajo families resided on land partitioned (or judicially confirmed) to the Hopi, while only 26 eligible Hopi families lived on Navajo partitioned land, according to ONHIR data. By the end of FY2005, according to ONHIR, 98% of the currently eligible Navajo families and 100% of the Hopi families had completed relocation. In addition, however, ONHIR estimates that about half of roughly 250 Navajo families (not all of them eligible families) who live on Hopi land and signed "accommodation agreements" (under P.L. 104-301) that allow them to stay on Hopi land, under Hopi law, may wish to opt out of these agreements and relocate using ONHIR benefits.

ONHIR estimated that, as of the end of FY2005, 83 eligible Navajo families were awaiting relocation. Eight of these 83 families still resided on Hopi partitioned land; one of these families was seeking a relocation home and the other seven refused to relocate or sign an accommodation agreement. ONHIR and the U.S. Department of Justice were negotiating with the Hopi Tribe to allow the seven families to stay on Hopi land, as autonomous families, in return for ONHIR's relocating off Hopi land those families who had signed accommodation agreements but later decided to opt out and accept relocation.

In its FY2007 budget justification ONHIR had estimated that relocation moves for currently eligible families would be completed by the end of FY2006. However, the addition of Navajo families who opt out of accommodation agreements and of Navajo families who filed late applications or appeals (but whom ONHIR proposes to accommodate to avoid litigation),[45] would mean that all relocation moves would not be completed until the end of FY2008, according to ONHIR. This schedule for completion of relocations would depend on infrastructure needs and relocatees' decisions. In addition, required post-move assistance to relocatees would necessitate another two years of expenditures after the last relocation move (whether in FY2006 or FY2008).

Congress has been concerned, at times, about the speed of the relocation process and about avoiding forced relocations or evictions. In the 109th Congress, legislation passed the Senate, but not the House, to sunset ONHIR in 2008 and transfer any remaining duties to the Secretary of the Interior. Further, a long-standing proviso in ONHIR appropriations language, retained for FY2008, prohibits ONHIR from evicting any Navajo family from Hopi partitioned lands unless a replacement home were provided. This language appears to prevent ONHIR from forcibly relocating Navajo families, because of ONHIR's backlog of approved relocatees awaiting replacement homes. As the backlog is reduced, however, forced eviction may become an issue, if any remaining Navajo families were to refuse relocation and if the Hopi Tribe were to exercise a right under P.L. 104-301 to begin legal action against the United States for failure to give the Hopi Tribe "quiet possession" of all Hopi partitioned lands. The purpose of the negotiations among ONHIR, the Justice Department, and the Hopi Tribe, mentioned above, was to avoid this.

SMITHSONIAN INSTITUTION

The Smithsonian Institution (SI) is a museum and research complex consisting of 19 museums and galleries and the National Zoo in addition to 9 research facilities throughout the United States and around the world. Smithsonian facilities logged nearly 23 million visitors in 2006. Established by federal legislation in 1846 in acceptance of a trust donation by the Institution's namesake benefactor, SI is funded by both federal appropriations and a private trust, with over $979 million in revenue for FY2006.[46] The FY2008 appropriations law provided $682.6 million for SI, an increase of $47.7 million (8%) over the FY2007 level of $634.9 million and of $4.2 million (<1%) over the Administration's request of $678.4 million. See table 19. Funding was provided for three main line items: Salaries and Expenses, Facilities Capital, and a new Legacy Fund.

Salaries and Expenses

For FY2008, the Smithsonian was appropriated $562.4 million to fund Salaries and Expenses for its museums, research centers, and administration. FY2008 funding represented a $26.1 million (5%) increase over FY2007 ($536.3 million) but an $8.9 million (2%) decrease from the President's requested level ($571.3 million). The growth over FY2007 in staff and expenditures would primarily be for the National Museum of African American History and Culture (established by P.L. 108-184), which is under development. Federal appropriations fund salaries of over 4,200 employees.

During consideration of FY2008 Interior appropriations legislation, concerns were raised by the Appropriations Committees and other Members over governance and fiscal management at the Smithsonian. Questions over the salary[47] and other compensation for Smithsonian Secretary Lawrence M. Small led to his resignation in March 2007. Subsequently, the Deputy Secretary also resigned in 2007, as did the chief executive officer of Smithsonian Business Ventures amid an investigation of his expenses. In addition to the changes in senior leadership, the Smithsonian Board of Regents began an effort to reform governance and oversight at the Institution. In the explanatory statement accompanying the FY2008 funding act, the Appropriations Committees expressed "increased confidence" in SI for these efforts, but noted that the Committees will continue to carefully monitor progress (Explanatory Statement, H16140).

Facilities Capital

The SI is responsible for over 400 buildings with approximately 8 million square feet of space. Recent external studies[48] and the SI estimate that an investment of $2.3 billion over ten years is needed to address advanced facilities deterioration. Recent appropriations and fundraising fall far short of this level. The FY2008 law provided $105.4 million for Facilities Capital, with the bulk of the funds for renovations and the balance for security and health and safety improvements. This was an increase over FY2007 of $6.8 million (7%) but a decrease of $1.7 million (2%) from the Administration's request. No funds for construction were appropriated for FY2008.

Trust Funds

In addition to federal appropriations, the Smithsonian Institution receives income from trust funds which support salaries for some employees, donor-designated capital projects and exhibits, and operations. At the end of FY2006, the SI trust funds endowment was valued at over $2.2 billion. Non-appropriated revenues fund over a third of SI operations and include income from the trusts, contributions from private sources, competitive government grants and contracts from other agencies, and the profits from the Smithsonian Business Ventures division. For FY2008, the SI estimates $284.1 million will be available for Institution operations from these sources.

Table 19. Appropriations for the Smithsonian Institution, FY2007-FY2008 ($ in thousands)

Smithsonian Institution	FY2007 Approp.	FY2008 Request	FY2008 House Passed	FY2008 Senate Comm.	FY2008 Approp.
Salaries and Expenses	536,295	571,347	536,295	571,705	562,434
— Museums and Research Institutes	215,195	231,541	231,541	231,541	227,929
— Program Support and Outreach	37,567	38,205	38,205	38,205	37,609
— Administration	64,110	66,740	66,740	66,991	65,699
— Inspector General	1,834	1,977	1,977	2084	1,946
— Facilities Services	217,589	232,884	232,884	232,884	229,251
— General Reduction[a]	—	—	-35,052	—	—
Facilities Capital	98,600	107,100	116,100	125,000	105,429
— Revitalization	82,700	91,400	100,400	109,000	89,974
— Construction	5,400	0	0	0	0
— Facilities Planning and Design	10,500	15,700	15,700	16,000	15,455
Legacy Fund	—	—	—	15,000	14,766
Total Appropriations	634,895	678,447	652,395	696,705	682,629

a. The allocation of the recommended "general reduction" within activities covered by Salaries and Expenses was not specified.

Legacy Fund

The FY2008 law included a new account — not provided for by either the House or Senate Appropriations Committee bills — called the Legacy

Fund. The Fund's purpose is to address the backlog of facilities capital repairs. For FY2008, up to $14.8 million in federal funding was provided for the initiative, with a requirement that private dollars match each federal dollar two to one.

For further information on the *Smithsonian Institution*, see its website at [http://www.si.edu/].

NATIONAL ENDOWMENT FOR THE ARTS AND NATIONAL ENDOWMENT FOR THE HUMANITIES

One of the primary vehicles for federal support for the arts and the humanities is the National Foundation on the Arts and the Humanities, composed of the National Endowment for the Arts (NEA), the National Endowment for the Humanities (NEH), the Federal Council on the Arts and Humanities, and the Institute of Museum and Library Services (IMLS).[49] The NEA and NEH authorization (P.L. 89-209; 20 U.S.C. §951) expired at the end of FY1993, but the agencies have been operating on temporary authority through appropriations law. The FY2008 law provided a total of $289.4 million to the arts and humanities — an increase of $23.7 million (9%) over FY2007. The Administration had requested $269.8 million, and the FY2008 appropriation was an increase of $19.6 million (7%) over that amount.

NEA

The NEA is a major federal source of support for all arts disciplines. Since 1965 it has provided over 120,000 grants that have been distributed to all states. For FY2008, the NEA was funded at $144.7 million, an increase of $20.1 million (16%) over FY2007, as shown in table 20. The House bill had included a substantial increase for the agency (28%); the House had considered, but did not agree to, several floor amendments to cut or eliminate funding for the arts. Floor amendments to increase or decrease arts funding similarly have been raised for many years. The Senate committee recommendation for FY2008 would have provided a smaller increase over FY2007 of 7%. Within NEA grants, the final law included $9.3 million to fund Challenge America — a program of matching grants for arts education, outreach, and community arts activities for rural and under-served areas. The

FY2008 law also provided $13.3 million in grants for *American Masterpieces* — touring programs, local presentations, and arts education in the fields of dance, visual arts, and music.

Table 20. Appropriations for Arts and Humanities, FY2007-FY2008 ($ in thousands)

Arts and Humanities	FY2007 Approp.	FY2008 Request	FY2008 House Passed	FY2008 Senate Comm.	FY2008 Approp.
National Endowment for the Arts					
Grants	100,319	102,942	133,500	107,942	119,604
Program Support	1,672	1,636	2,000	1,636	1,673
Administration	22,571	23,834	24,500	23,834	23,429
Subtotal, NEA	124,562	128,412	160,000	133,412	144,706
National Endowment for the Humanities					
Grants	102,247	101,807	119,900	106,807	105,731
Matching Grants	15,221	14,510	14,500	14,510	14,284
Administration	23,637	25,038	25,600	25,038	24,692
Subtotal, NEH	141,105	141,355	160,000	146,355	144,707
Total NEA and NEH	265,667	269,767	320,000	279,767	289,413

NEH

The NEH generally supports grants for humanities education, research, preservation and public humanities programs; the creation of regional humanities centers; and development of humanities programs under the jurisdiction of the 56 state humanities councils. Since 1965, NEH has provided approximately 61,000 grants. NEH also supports a Challenge Grant program to stimulate and match private donations in support of humanities institutions. For FY2008, NEH requested $141.4 million, essentially level with FY2007. The FY2008 law provided $144.7 million, an increase of $3.6 million (3%) above FY2007. Both the House and the Senate committee bills had supported larger increases over FY2007 — 13% and 4% respectively. The two largest grant programs funded by NEH are federal/state partnership grants and the *We the People Initiative* grants, funded at $31.7 million and $15.0 million in the FY2008 law, respectively. *We the People* grants include model curriculum projects for schools to improve course offerings in the humanities. FY2007 program funding was $30.9 million for federal/state partnerships and $15.2 million for We the People.

For further information on the *National Endowment for the Arts*, see its website at [http://arts.endow.gov/].

For further information on the *National Endowment for the Humanities*, see its website at [http://www.neh.gov/].

CRS Report RS20287. Arts and Humanities: Background on Funding, by Susan Boren.

Chapter 7

CROSS-CUTTING TOPICS

THE LAND AND WATER CONSERVATION FUND (LWCF)

Overview

The LWCF (16 U.S.C. §§460*l*-4, et seq.) is authorized at $900 million annually through FY2015. However, these funds may not be spent without an appropriation. The LWCF is used for three purposes. First, the four principal federal land management agencies — Bureau of Land Management, Fish and Wildlife Service, National Park Service, and Forest Service — draw primarily on the LWCF to acquire lands. The sections on each of those agencies earlier in this report identify funding levels and other details for their land acquisition activities. Second, the LWCF funds acquisition and recreational development by state and local governments through a grant program administered by the NPS, sometimes referred to as stateside funding. Third, Administrations have requested, and Congress has appropriated, money from the LWCF to fund some related activities. This third use is relatively recent, starting with the FY1998 appropriation. Programs funded have varied from year to year. Most of the appropriations for federal acquisitions generally are specified for management units, such as a specific National Wildlife Refuge. The appropriations for the state grant program and other related activities rarely have been specified for individual projects or areas.

From FY1965 through FY2007, about $30 billion was credited to the LWCF. About half that amount — $15 billion — has been appropriated. Throughout history, annual appropriations from LWCF have fluctuated considerably. Until FY1998, LWCF funding did not exceed $400 million, except from FY1977-FY1980, when funding was between $509 million and $805 million. In FY1998, LWCF appropriations exceeded the authorized level for the first time, spiking to $969 million from the FY1997 level of $159 million. A record level of funding was provided in FY2001, when appropriations reached $1.0 billion, partly in response to President Clinton's Lands Legacy Initiative and some interest in increased and more certain funding for LWCF.

FY2008 Funding

For FY2008, the total LWCF appropriation was $255.5 million. This was a $110.4 million (30%) reduction from FY2007 ($365.9 million), as well as a $123.2 million (33%) reduction from the Administration's request for FY2008 ($378.7 million). Both the House and the Senate Appropriations Committee had supported decreases from the FY2007 level. The Senate committee had recommended $292.9 million for LWCF, while the House had approved $261.9 million. The FY2008 law included an additional $7.7 million for land appraisals related to federal land acquisitions, but it did not appear that this amount would be derived from LWCF. The FY2008 appropriated level included funds for federal land acquisition, the stateside program, and other purposes as described below.

Land Acquisition

For land acquisition, the FY2008 law contained $129.7 million for land acquisition, a $16.7 million (15%) increase over FY2007 ($113.0 million) and more than double the Administration's request for FY2008. The House and the Senate Appropriations Committee had supported higher funding. The House had approved $155.6 million, with an additional $7.8 million for land appraisals apparently not derived from LWCF. The Senate Appropriations Committee had recommended $152.2 million for land acquisition, and $7.8 million for land appraisals with funds derived from LWCF.

For the five fiscal years ending in FY2001, appropriations for federal land acquisition had more than tripled, rising from $136.6 million in FY1996 to $453.4 million in FY2001. The appropriation for land acquisition has subsequently declined to roughly the FY1996 level — to $129.7 million for FY2008. The decline may be attributed in part to increased interest in allocating funding to lands already in federal ownership, reducing the federal budget deficit, and funding other national priorities, such as the war on terrorism. Table 21 shows recent funding for LWCF.

Table 21. Appropriations from the Land and Water Conservation Fund, FY2004-FY2008 ($ in millions)

Land and Water Conservation Fund	FY2004 Approp.	FY2005 Approp.	FY2006 Approp.	FY2007 Approp.	FY2008 Request	FY2008 House Passed	FY2008 Senate Comm.	FY2008 Approp.
Federal Acquisition								
—BLM	18.4	11.2	8.6	8.6	1.6	18.6	12.2	8.9
—FWS	38.1	37.0	28.0	28.0	18.0	43.0	43.0	34.6
—NPS	41.7	55.1	17.4[a]	34.4	22.5	49.4	48.7	44.4
—FS	66.4	61.0	41.9	41.9	15.7	44.5	48.2	41.8
Subtotal, Federal Acquisition	164.6	164.3	95.8	113.0	57.9	155.6	152.2	129.7
Appraisal Services[c]	0.0	0.0	7.3	7.4	7.8	0.0	7.8	0.0
Grants to States	93.8	91.2	29.6	29.6	0.0[b]	50.0	30.0	24.6
Other Programs	229.7	203.4	213.1	215.9	313.1	56.3	102.9	101.1
Total Appropriations	488.1	458.9	345.9	365.9	378.7	261.9	292.9	255.5

Source: Data are from the House and Senate Appropriations Committees, the DOI Budget Office, and The Interior Budget in Brief for each fiscal year.

a. This figure does not reflect the availability of an additional $26.8 million in prior year funds.

b. The President proposed $1.4 million for the administration of state grants in FY2008, to be derived from the appropriation for National Recreation and Preservation rather than the LWCF. Accordingly, this amount is not reflected here.

c. For FY2008, for appraisal services the House approved $7.8 million, and the law contained $7.7 million, but it does not appear that these amounts were to be derived from LWCF. Accordingly, they are not reflected here.

Grants to States

For FY2008, $24.6 million was appropriated for the stateside program, comprised of $23.1 million for new stateside grants and $1.5 million for administrative expenses. That figure was $5.0 million (17%) less than appropriated for FY2007 ($29.6 million). The Senate Appropriations Committee had recommended funding at about the FY2007 level ($30.0 million), but the House had approved a substantial increase (to $50.0 million).

The Administration did not request funds for new stateside grants in FY2008, as in FY2006 and FY2007. The Administration has asserted that state and local governments have alternative sources of funding for parkland acquisition and development, and that the current program could not adequately measure performance or demonstrate results. As for FY2006 and FY2007, for FY2008 the Administration did request a relatively small amount of funding for administration of the grant program. Specifically, the Administration supported $1.4 million for program administration in FY2008, but in a break from the past, the Administration asked that the funds be derived from the National Recreation and Preservation line item rather than the LWCF. Seeking to eliminate funds for new stateside grants is not a new phenomenon. For example, for several years the Clinton Administration proposed eliminating stateside funding, and Congress concurred. In the last seven years, stateside funding has fallen 83%, from $143.9 million in FY2002 to $24.6 million in FY2007.

Through provisions of the Gulf of Mexico Energy Security Act of 2006 (P.L. 109-432), a portion of revenues from certain OCS leasing will be provided in future years (without further appropriation) to the stateside grant program. No money is expected to be available under these provisions for FY2008. An estimated $6.4 million in revenue from such OCS leasing is projected to be collected in FY2008 and disbursed to the stateside program in FY2009. Preliminary estimates of disbursements through FY2017 total approximately $21.8 million, according to the DOI Budget Office.

Table 22. Appropriations for Other Programs from the LWCF, FY2006-FY2008 ($ in millions)

Other Programs	FY2006 Approp.	FY2007 Approp.	FY2008 Request	FY2008 House Passed	FY2008 Senate Comm.	FY2008 Approp.
Department of the Interior						
Bureau of Land Management						
— Challenge Cost Share	0.0	0.0	9.4	0.0	0.0	0.0
Fish and Wildlife Service						
— Refuge Challenge Cost Share	0.0	0.0	6.7	0.0	0.0	0.0
— Partners for Fish and Wildlife	0.0	0.0	48.4	0.0	0.0	0.0
— Coastal Programs	0.0	0.0	13.3	0.0	0.0	0.0
— Migratory Bird Joint Ventures	0.0	0.0	11.1	0.0	0.0	0.0
— State and Tribal Wildlife	67.5	67.5	69.5	0.0	0.0	0.0
Grants						
— Landowner Incentive Grants	21.7	23.7	0.0	0.0	0.0	0.0
— Private Stewardship Grants	7.3	7.3	0.0	0.0	0.0	0.0
— Cooperative Endangered	60.1	61.1	80.0	0.0	54.8	48.9
Species Grants						
— North American Wetlands Conservation Fund Grants	0.0	0.0	42.6	0.0	0.0	0.0
National Park Service						
— Challenge Cost Share	0.0	0.0	2.4	0.0	0.0	0.0
Departmental Management						
— Take Pride in America	0.0	0.0	0.5	0.0	0.0	0.0
Forest Service (USDA)						
— Forest Legacy Program	56.5	56.3	29.3	56.3	48.1	52.2
Total Appropriations	213.1	215.9	313.1	56.3	102.9	101.1

Notes: This table identifies "other" programs for which Congress appropriated funds for FY2006 through FY2008. It excludes federal land acquisition and the stateside program. Funding provided outside of LWCF is not reflected. Information is from the DOI Budget Office and House and Senate Appropriations Committees.

Other Purposes. The FY2008 law provided funding from LWCF for two other programs, for a total of $101.1 million. Of the total, $48.9 million was provided for Cooperative Endangered Species Grants and $52.2 million was for the Forest Legacy Program. The Senate Appropriations Committee also had sought funding for these two programs from LWCF, for a total of $102.9 million. The House had approved funding only for Forest Legacy — $56.3 million. By contrast, the President had sought funding for 11 other programs in the Department of the Interior and the Forest Service. The largest portion of the President's FY2008 LWCF request — $313.1 million — was for these other programs. The FY2008 appropriation for other programs was less than half that provided in FY2007, when $215.9 million was appropriated for five programs. Table 21 shows that for each year from FY2004 through FY2007, the largest portion of the LWCF appropriation was for other programs. This changed in FY2008, when the largest portion of the LWCF appropriation was for land acquisition. The Administration had requested a much larger amount than was appropriated for each year for other programs, for instance requesting $440.6 million for FY2007.

Table 22 shows the other programs for which Congress appropriated funds for FY2006 through FY2008. In some cases, Congress provided these programs with non-LWCF funding, which is not reflected here.

CRS Report RL33531. Land and Water Conservation Fund: Overview, Funding History, and Current Issues, by Carol Hardy Vincent.

Everglades Restoration

Altered natural flows of water by a series of canals, levees, and pumping stations, combined with agricultural and urban development, are thought to be the leading causes of environmental deterioration in South Florida. In 1996, Congress authorized the U.S. Army Corps of Engineers (Corps) to create a comprehensive plan to restore, protect, and preserve the entire South Florida ecosystem, which includes the Everglades (P.L. 104-303). A portion of this plan, the Comprehensive Everglades Restoration Plan (CERP), was completed in 1999, and provides for federal involvement in restoring the ecosystem. Congress authorized the Corps to implement CERP in Title IV of the Water Resources Development Act of 2000 (WRDA 2000, P.L. 106-541). While restoration activities in the South Florida ecosystem are conducted under several federal laws, WRDA 2000 is considered the seminal law for Everglades restoration.

Appropriations for restoration projects in the South Florida ecosystem have been provided to various agencies as part of several annual appropriations bills. The Interior, Environment, and Related Agencies appropriations laws have provided funds to several DOI agencies for restoration projects. Specifically, DOI conducts CERP and non-CERP activities in southern Florida through the National Park Service, Fish and Wildlife Service, U.S. Geological Survey, and Bureau of Indian Affairs.

From FY1993 to FY2007, federal appropriations for projects and services related to the restoration of the South Florida ecosystem exceeded $2.8 billion, and state funding topped $4.8 billion.[50] The average annual federal cost for restoration activities in southern Florida in the next 10 years is expected to be approximately $286 million per year.[51] For FY2008, the Administration requested $235.0 million for DOI and the Corps for restoration efforts in the Everglades.

FY2008 Funding

It is generally not possible to identify specific funding amounts for Everglades restoration activities from enacted appropriations laws and their explanatory statements. Accordingly, they are not reflected for FY2008 in Table 23. However, funds for the Modified Water Deliveries Project were specified in the FY2008 law, and are discussed below. Other specific funding amounts for Everglades restoration under DOI will be available in the FY2009 Administration's request.

The FY2008 law provided $14.3 million for Mod Waters under NPS construction. This project is designed to improve water deliveries to Everglades National Park, and to the extent possible, restore the natural hydrological conditions within the Park. The completion of this project is required prior to the construction of certain projects under CERP. For FY2007, $13.3 million in new funds were appropriated for Mod Waters. For FY2008, $14.5 million was requested and provided in the House and the Senate committee bills. The House Appropriations Committee noted that it intends to monitor the progress of restoring the Everglades and requested that the DOI submit a progress report on the status of restoration (H.Rept. 110-187, p. 44). The FY2008 law provided funds for Mod Waters under NPS construction only if matching amounts are appropriated for similar purposes to the Corps. Further, the FY2008 law prohibited funding for Mod Waters under NPS Construction if any Corps matching funds for Mod Waters become unavailable, including funds for design analysis of the

Tamiami Trail (a component of Mod Waters). Funds for evaluating Tamiami Trail were provided to the Corps in the FY2008 law. Also, the law provided $9.8 million to the Corps for Mod Waters. Because this is less than the level appropriated to the NPS, it is uncertain if NPS funding will be decreased to match Corps funding.

Table 23. Appropriations for Everglades Restoration in the DOI Budget, FY2007-FY2008 ($ in thousands)

Everglades Restoration in DOI	FY2007 Approp.	FY2008 Request
National Park Service		
— CERP	4,658	4,731
— Park Operations[a]	26,350	28,991
— Land Acquisition (use of prior year balances)	0	0
— Everglades Acquisitions Management	500	500
— Modified Water Delivery	13,330	14,526
— Everglades Research	3,863	3,910
— South Florida Ecosystem Task Force	1,308	1,324
— GSA Space	554	554
Subtotal, NPS	50,563	54,536
Fish and Wildlife Service		
— CERP	3,269	3,269
— Land Acquisition	0	1,044
— Ecological Services	2,516	2,516
— Refuges and Wildlife	4,086	4,086
— Migratory Birds	101	101
— Law Enforcement	619	619
— Fisheries	95	95
Subtotal, FWS	10,686	11,730
U.S. Geological Survey		
— Research, Planning and Coordination	7,771	5,771
Subtotal, USGS	7,771	5,771
Bureau of Indian Affairs		
— Seminole, Miccosukee Tribe Water Studies and	382	382
Restoration		
Subtotal, BIA	382	382
Total Appropriations	69,402	72,419

Source: U.S. Department of the Interior, *Fiscal Year 2008, The Interior Budget in Brief* (Washington, DC: February 2007).

[a]. This includes total funding for park operations in Everglades National Park, Dry Tortugas National Park, Biscayne National Park, and Big Cypress National Preserve.

A funding issue receiving broad attention is the level of commitment by the federal government to implement restoration activities in the Everglades. Some observers measure commitment by the frequency and number of projects authorized under CERP, and the appropriations they receive. Because no restoration projects have been authorized since WRDA 2000, these observers are concerned that federal commitment to CERP implementation is waning. Others assert that the federal commitment will be measurable by the amount of federal funding for construction, expected when the first projects break ground in the next few years. Some state and federal officials contend that federal funding will increase compared to state funding as CERP projects move beyond design into construction. Still others question whether the federal government should maintain the current level of funding, or increase its commitment, because of escalating costs and project delays.

Concerns over Phosphorus Mitigation

Since FY2004, Interior appropriations laws have conditioned funding for the Modified Water Deliveries Project based on meeting state water quality standards. Funds appropriated in the laws and any prior laws for Mod Waters would be provided *unless* administrators of four federal departments/agencies (Secretary of the Interior, Secretary of the Army, Administrator of the EPA, and the Attorney General) indicate in their joint report that water entering the A.R.M. Loxahatchee National Wildlife Refuge and Everglades National Park do not meet state water quality standards, and the House and Senate Committees on Appropriations respond in writing disapproving the further expenditure of funds. These provisions were enacted based on concerns regarding a Florida state law (Chapter 2003-12, enacted on May 20, 2003) that amended the Everglades Forever Act of 1994 (Florida Statutes §373.4592) by authorizing a new plan to mitigate phosphorus pollution in the Everglades. Phosphorus is one of the primary water pollutants in the Everglades and a primary cause for ecosystem degradation. Provisions conditioning funds on the achievement of water quality standards are included in the FY2008 appropriations law.

For further information on *Everglades Restoration*, see the website of the South Florida Ecosystem Restoration Program at [http://www.sfrestore.org] and the website of the Corps of Engineers at [http://www.evergladesplan.org/].

Table 24. Appropriations for Interior, Environment, and Related Agencies, FY2004-FY2008 ($ in thousands)

Bureau or Agency	FY2004 Approp.	FY2005 Approp.	FY2006 Approp.[g]	FY2007 Approp.	FY2008 Request	FY2008 House Passed	FY2008 Senate Comm.	FY2008 Approp.
Title I: Department of the Interior								
Bureau of Land Management	1,893,233	1,816,910	1,757,188	1,872,047	1,822,029	1,853,029	1,888,736	1,808,245[n]
U.S. Fish and Wildlife Service	1,308,405	1,332,591	1,307,639	1,338,109	1,286,769	1,417,120	1,380,857	1,366,226
National Park Service	2,258,581	2,365,683	2,255,768	2,299,960	2,363,784	2,513,172	2,461,419	2,390,359
U.S. Geological Survey	937,985	944,564	961,675	988,050	974,952	1,032,764	1,009,933	1,006,482
Minerals Management Service	170,297	173,826	158,294	159,515	161,451	66,955	166,351	115,933
Office of Surface Mining Reclamation and Enforcement	295,975	296,573	294,228	294,591	168,295	170,211	174,295	170,411
Bureau of Indian Affairs	2,300,814	2,295,702	2,274,270	2,308,304	2,228,890	2,346,940	2,265,698	2,291,279
Departmental Offices[a]	460,859	496,837	527,656	514,873	478,657	486,681	486,302	474,232
Department-Wide Programs[b]	221,815	232,542	248,254	248,286	228,418	268,854	285,851	284,994
Total Title I	9,847,964	9,955,228	9,784,972	10,023,735	9,713,245	10,155,726	10,119,442	9,908,161
Title II: Environmental Protection Agency	8,365,817d	8,026,485	7,617,416	7,725,130	7,199,400	8,090,915	7,772,928	7,461,494

Table 24. (Continued).

Bureau or Agency	FY2004 Approp.	FY2005 Approp.	FY2006 Approp.[g]	FY2007 Approp.	FY2008 Request	FY2008 House Passed	FY2008 Senate Comm.	FY2008 Approp.
Title III: Related Agencies								
U.S. Forest Service[e]	4,939,899	4,770,598	4,200,762	4,706,349	4,126,873	4,577,514	4,549,543	4,447,921
Indian Health Service	2,921,715	2,985,066	3,045,310	3,180,148	3,270,726	3,384,427	3,367,399	3,346,182
National Institute of Environmental Health Sciences	78,309	79,842	79,108	79,117	78,434	79,117	78,434	77,546
Agency for Toxic Substances and Disease Registry	73,034	76,041	74,905	75,212	75,004	75,212	75,004	74,039
Council on Environmental Quality and Office of Environmental Quality	3,219	3,258	2,677	2,698	2,703	2,703	2,703	2,661
Chemical Safety and Hazard Investigation Board	8,648	9,424	9,064	9,113	9,049	9,549	9,049	9,263
Office of Navajo and Hopi Indian Relocation	13,366	4,930	8,474	8,509	9,000	9,000	9,000	8,860

Table 24. (Continued).

Bureau or Agency	FY2004 Approp.	FY2005 Approp.	FY2006 Approp.g	FY2007 Approp.	FY2008 Request	FY2008 House Passed	FY2008 Senate Comm.	FY2008 Approp.
Institute of American Indian and Alaska Native Culture and Arts Development	6,173	5,916	6,207	6,207	7,297	7,297	7,297	7,183
Smithsonian Institution	596,279	615,158	615,097	634,895	678,447	652,395	696,705	682,629
National Gallery of Art	98,225	102,654	111,141	111,729	116,000	119,867	119,735	117,866
John F. Kennedy Center for the Performing Arts	32,159	33,021	30,347	30,389	39,350	43,350	43,350	42,674
Woodrow Wilson International Center for Scholars	8,498	8,863	9,065	9,100	8,857	10,000	9,718	9,844
National Endowment for the Arts	120,972	121,264	124,406	124,562	128,412	160,000	133,412	144,706
National Endowment for the Humanities	135,310	138,054	140,949	141,105	141,355	160,000	146,355	144,707
Commission of Fine Arts	1,405	1,768	1,865	1,873	2,092	2,092	2,192	2,059
National Capital Arts and Cultural Affairs	6,914	6,902	7,143	7,143	—	10,000	7,200	8,367
Advisory Council on Historic Preservation	3,951	4,536	4,789	4,828	5,348	5,348	5,348	5,265

Table 24. (Continued).

Bureau or Agency	FY2004 Approp.	FY2005 Approp.	FY2006 Approp.g	FY2007 Approp.	FY2008 Request	FY2008 House Passed	FY2008 Senate Comm.	FY2008 Approp.
National Capital Planning Commission	7,635	7,888	8,123	8,168	8,265	8,265	8,265	8,136
U.S. Holocaust Memorial Museum	39,505	40,858	42,150	42,349	44,996	44,996	45,496	44,786
Presidio Trust	20,445	19,722	19,706	19,706	18,450	22,400	18,450	22,051
White House Commission on the Natl. Moment of Remembrance	—	248	247	247	200	200	200	197
Dwight D. Eisenhower Memorial Comm.	—	—	—	—	5,000	—	—	1,969
Total Title III	9,115,661	9,036,011	8,541,535	9,203,447	8,775,858	9,383,732	9,334,855	9,208,911
[Title IV: Veterans' Health]	—	—	*[1,500,000]*	—	—	—	—	—
Title IV: Secure Rural Schools	—	—	—	425,000	—	—	—	—
Title V: Wildfire Suppression Emergency Appropriations	—	—	—	—	—	—	—	300,0001
Grand Total (in Bill)c	*27,329,442*	*27,017,724*	*25,942,155 f*	*27,377,312 h*	*25,688,503*	*27,631,373 i*	*27,186,125 j*	27,391,125 k

Table 24. (Continued).

Source: House and Senate Appropriations Committees.

[a] The Departmental Offices figure currently includes the Office of the Secretary, Insular Affairs, Office of the Solicitor, Office of Inspector General, and Office of Special Trustee for American Indians.

[b] The Department-Wide Programs figure currently includes the Payments in Lieu of Taxes Program (PILT), Central Hazardous Materials Fund, Natural Resource Damage Assessment Fund, and Working Capital Fund.

[c] Figures generally do not reflect scorekeeping adjustments.

[d] Derived from the report of the House Appropriations Committee on H.R. 5041 (H.Rept. 108-674).

[e] The FY2005 figure excludes $40.0 million in transferred funds from the Department of Defense (§8098, P.L. 108-287). The FY2008 total excludes appropriations in Title V of P.L. 110-161, and appropriations in P.L. 110-116. With these additional appropriations, the FS total was $5.0 billion for FY2008.

[f] The total does not include supplemental appropriations or $1.50 billion in emergency appropriations for veteran's health. It reflects $1.8 million in undistributed reductions which are not reflected in the individual agency figures in the column.

[g] Supplemental appropriations are not reflected in this column.

[h] The total includes $425.0 million in emergency appropriations for Secure Rural Schools.

[i] The total reflects a $1.0 million increase from Forest Service rights of way.

[j] The total reflects a reduction for Minerals Management Service state royalty costs, and increases from Forest Service marina fees and rights-of- way.

[k] The total reflects an appropriation of $26.89 billion in P.L. 110-161, the Consolidated Appropriations Act for FY2008, and an appropriation of $0.5 billion in emergency supplemental funding in P.L. 110-116. It further reflects several adjustments totaling $12.6 million that are not reflected in the individual agency figures in this column.

[l] Of this total, $78.0 million was appropriated to the Bureau of Land Management and $222.0 million was appropriated to the Forest Service.

[m] These funds were provided for emergency wildland fire management. Of this total, $171.0 million was appropriated to the Bureau of Land Management and $329.0 million was appropriated to the Forest Service.

[n] The FY2008 total excludes appropriations in Title V of P.L. 110-161, and appropriations in P.L. 110-116. With these additional appropriations, the BLM total was $2.06 billion for FY2008.

CRS Report RS22048. *Everglades Restoration: The Federal Role in Funding*, by Pervaze A. Sheikh and Nicole T. Carter.

CRS Report RS21331. Everglades Restoration: Modified Water Deliveries Project, by Pervaze A. Sheikh.

CRS Report RS20702. South Florida Ecosystem Restoration and the Comprehensive Everglades Restoration Plan, by Pervaze A. Sheikh and Nicole T. Carter.

REFERENCES

[1] These panels are now called the Subcommittees on Energy and Water Development.

[2] These panels are now called the Subcommittees on Interior, Environment, and Related Agencies.

[3] In addition, final FY2007 enacted levels are not included in CRS Report RL33399, *Interior, Environment, and Related Agencies: FY2007 Appropriations*, because they were not available until after the start of the 110th Congress and the beginning of the FY2008 appropriations cycle.

[4] *Congressional Record*, v. 153, December 17, 2007, Book II, Explanatory Statement, Division F, Sec. 433, p. H16141-H16142. Hereafter cited as "Explanatory Statement," with the *Congressional Record* page number.

[5] Under the Migratory Bird Conservation Account (MBCA), FWS has a permanently appropriated source of mandatory funding (from the sale of duck stamps to hunters, and import duties on certain arms and ammunition) for land acquisition. As annual appropriations for acquisitions under LWCF have declined, the MBCA ($41.9 million in FY2006) has become increasingly important in the protection of habitat for migratory birds, especially waterfowl. Other species in these habitats benefit incidentally.

[6] The President's FY2008 budget did not propose to move funding for NMBCF into the MSCF. Congress had rejected the Administration's proposed transfer for the previous six fiscal years, beginning in FY2002.

[7] See the website of the National Parks Conservation Association at [http://www.npca.org/ media_center/reports/analysis.html].

[8] This information is from discussions with Walter Cruickshank, Deputy Director of MMS, during April 2006.

[9] For more information, see CRS Report RS22567, Royalty Relief for U.S. Deepwater Oil and Gas Leases, by Marc Humphries and CRS Report RL33974 Legal Issues Raised by Provision in House Energy Bill (H.R. 6) Creating Incentives for Certain OCS Leaseholders to Accept Price Thresholds, by Robert Meltz and Adam Vann.

[10] The report of the panel, *Mineral Revenue Collection from Federal and Indian Lands and the Outer Continental Shelf,* is available on the MMS website at [http://www.mrm.mms.gov/ Laws_R_D/RoyPC/ PdFDocs/RPCRMS1207.pdf].

[11] The regulations on suspension are at 30 C.F.R §250.168.

[12] California v. Norton, 150 F.Supp.2d 1046 (N.D. Cal. 2001).

[13] California v. Norton, 311 F.3d 1162 (9th Cir. 2002).

[14] Amber Resources Co. v. U.S., 68 Fed. Cl. 535 (2005).

[15] Id. at 546-48.

[16] Id. at 560. The lessees continued to pursue further recovery under other breach of contract theories. These matters remain unsettled. *See* Amber Resources Corp. v. United States, 73 Fed. Cl. 738 (2006).

[17] Interest generated by unappropriated balances in the AML fund is transferred to the United Mine Workers of America Combined Benefit Fund, established by P.L. 102-486 to cover the unreimbursed health cost requirements of retired miners.

[18] The permanent appropriation has a ceiling of $490 million annually. If demands on that money, which include annual payments to the United Mine Workers of America Combined Benefit Fund, would exceed the cap, distributions will be proportional.

[19] Added to these totals will be any money needed to fund minimum program states. These states have sites remaining with serious problems. However, these states also have insufficient levels of current coal production to generate significant fees to the AML fund. Each minimum program state is to receive $1.5 million annually.

[20] Payments will be ramped up. For the first three years, certified states will receive 25%, 50%, and 75% of the amount the state would receive under the restructured program.

[21] An allocation of fee collections under the old program to the Rural Abandoned Mine Program (RAMP) is discontinued by P.L. 109-432, which transfers the RAMP balances to the fund pool representing state historical coal production. Whether or not fee collections are

reauthorized beyond FY2021, mandatory distributions will continue so long as money remains in the AML fund.

[22] In August 2006, the BIA's administrative office for its education programs was removed from the BIA, made a parallel agency under the Assistant Secretary — Indian Affairs, and renamed the Bureau of Indian Education (BIE). BIE appropriations remain within BIA appropriations.

[23] These sections are contained in 20 U.S.C. 6301 et seq. and 20 U.S.C. 7401 et seq. respectively.

[24] The tribal colleges and universities assistance statute limits the number of eligible tribally controlled colleges to one per tribe (25 U.S.C. 1801(a)(4)).

[25] The provision for tribally controlled vocational institutions is at 20 U.S.C. 2327.

[26] Testimony of Jefferson Keel, National Congress of American Indians, "NCAI Testimony on the Administration's Fiscal Year 2008 Budget Request for Indian Programs," presented at a hearing of the Senate Indian Affairs committee, Feb. 15, 2007, p. 3; available at [http://indian.senate.gov/public/_files/Keel021507.pdf].

[27] For further information on the BIA acknowledgment process, see CRS Report RS21109, The Bureau of Indian Affairs' Process for Recognizing Groups as Indian Tribes, by M. Maureen Murphy.

[28] See U.S. General Accounting Office, Indian Issues: Improvements Needed in Tribal Recognition Process (GAO-02-49, November 2001), and U.S. Government Accountability Office, Indian Issues: Timeliness of the Tribal Recognition Process Has Improved, But It Will Take Years to Clear the Existing Backlog of Petitions (GAO-05-347T, February 2005).

[29] This section addresses selected activities/offices that fall under *Departmental Offices* or *Department-Wide Programs*. Total funding for these entities is identified in Table 24 at the end of this book.

[30] When appropriations are not sufficient to cover the authorization, each county receives a pro rata share of the authorized amount.

[31] Figures are derived from the OST FY2008 Budget Justification.

[32] *Cobell v. Norton* (Civil No. 96-1285) (D.D.C.). Updated information is available on the websites of the plaintiffs at [http://www.indiantrust.com], the DOI at [http://www.doi.gov/indiantrust/], and the Justice Department at [http://www.usdoj.gov/civil/cases/cobell/index. htm].

[33] Testimony from the Interior Department estimated the cost at $12-$13 billion. See James Cason, Associate Deputy Secretary, U.S. Dept. of the Interior, Statement before the House Committee on Appropriations, Subcommittee on Interior, Environment, and Related Agencies, March 17, 2005. Previous Interior estimates of the cost were $6 billion-$12 billion.

[34] Trust Reform and Cobell Settlement Workgroup, "Principles for Legislation," June 20, 2005, p. 2, at [http://www.indiantrust.com/_pdfs/20050620SettlementPrinciples.pdf].

[35] The Judgment Fund is a permanent, indefinite appropriation for paying judgments against, and settlements by, the U.S. government. (See 31 U.S.C. §1304.)

[36] Matt Spangler, "Treasury Fund May Be Short of Cash Needed to Settle Indian Royalty Case," *Inside Energy with Federal Lands* (March 21, 2005), p. 6.

[37] See letter to Sen. Byron Dorgan, Chairman, Senate Indian Affairs committee, from the Secretary of the Interior and Attorney General, available at [http://www.indianz.com/docs/ cobell/bush030107.pdf].

[38] "Bush Administration Won't Admit Liability on Indian Trust," Indianz.com (March 30, 2007), available at [http://www.indianz.com/News/2007/002150.asp].

[39] Classes of Indian gaming were established by the IGRA, and NIGC has different but overlapping regulatory responsibilities for each class.

[40] EPA's funding was moved to the jurisdiction of the Interior Appropriations Subcommittees beginning with the FY2006 appropriations. In the beginning of the first session of the 109th Congress, the House and Senate Appropriations Committees abolished their respective Subcommittees on Veterans Affairs, Housing and Urban Development, and Independent Agencies, which previously had jurisdiction over EPA.

[41] See *Congressional Record*, December 17, 2007, H16131 — H16136. The amounts in the narrative of the explanatory statement do not reflect the 1.56% across-the-board rescission for discretionary accounts. However, the tables in the statement reflect the rescinded amounts. See H16168 — H16171.

[42] Congress established these accounts in FY1996 as a result of a restructuring of the agency's budget to more closely align the accounts with the purposes of the activities funded within them.

[43] 72 *Federal Register* 69, Jan. 3, 2007.

[44] See *Congressional Record*, December 17, 2007, House, H16133 — H16136. The dollar amounts indicated for each grant do not reflect the 1.56% across-the-board rescission. The disbursed amount of each grant also will depend on the amount of matching funds from the recipient.

[45] The number of families is estimated altogether at around 75; they overlap to an unpredicted extent with the 83 eligible Navajo families

[46] Smithsonian Institution, *Illumination: Annual Report 2006*. This and earlier annual reports are available online at [http://www.si.edu/opa/annualrpts/].

[47] Secretary Small was to receive $915,698 in 2007 (compared to the President's salary of $400,000). Some Members and others have questioned whether Congress should begin to limit the salaries and expenses of certain Smithsonian officials who are often compensated well over comparable federal levels because they are paid from private trust funds.

[48] For further information, see U.S. Government Accountability Office, *Smithsonian Institution: Facilities Management is Progressing, but Funding Remains a Challenge*, GAO-05-369 (April 2005).

[49] IMLS receives funding through the Departments of Labor, Health and Human Services, and Education, and Related Agencies Appropriations Acts.

[50] These figures represent an estimate of all CERP and non-CERP related costs for restoration in the South Florida ecosystem.

[51] This figure is based on CERP and non-CERP related restoration activities in South Florida.

INDEX

A

access, 35, 88
accidents, 41
accommodation, 90
accountability, 17
accounting, 10, 28, 58, 59, 60, 65, 87
achievement, 46, 105
acquisitions, 20, 24, 82, 97, 98, 113
adaptation, 72
administration, 17, 32, 92, 99, 100
administrators, 105
advocacy, 27
African American, 92
agricultural, 102
aid, 22, 31, 32
air pollution, 71
air quality, 63, 66, 71, 72
Alaska, 17, 23, 40, 46, 77, 83, 84, 87, 108
Alaska Natives, 83
alcohol, 86, 88
alternative, 38, 88, 100
alternative energy, 38
amendments, 9, 41, 42, 63, 69, 94
American History, 92
American Indian(s), viii, 9, 10, 46, 57, 58, 60, 83, 108, 110, 115
AML, 43, 44, 45, 114, 115
appraisals, 98
appropriations, vii, viii, 3, 4, 5, 6, 7, 8, 9, 13, 15, 16, 17, 18, 19, 21, 23, 24, 25, 26, 27, 29, 32, 38, 39, 40, 41, 43, 44, 46, 50, 51, 52, 53, 54, 55, 57, 59, 60, 61, 63, 65, 66, 67, 69, 70, 72, 73, 75, 76, 77, 79, 80, 82, 83, 85, 86, 87, 88, 89, 90, 91, 92, 93, 94, 97, 98, 103, 105, 110, 113, 115, 116
appropriations bills, vii, 26, 55, 76, 103
Appropriations Committee, 5, 9, 10, 15, 17, 18, 19, 20, 22, 23, 25, 27, 28, 30, 33, 36, 38, 40, 41, 45, 46, 50, 51, 52, 53, 54, 58, 59, 60, 61, 63, 64, 65, 66, 68, 69, 70, 71, 72, 75, 76, 78, 81, 83, 86, 87, 88, 90, 92, 93, 98, 99, 100, 101, 102, 103, 110, 116
Arctic National Wildlife Refuge, 26
argument, 50
Army Corps of Engineers, 102
Asia, 37
Asian, 23, 25
assessment, 34
assets, 46, 57, 58
assumptions, 56
attacks, 78
attention, 66, 105
Attorney General, 105, 116
auditing, 41
authority, 5, 6, 28, 29, 30, 32, 61, 94
availability, 41, 68, 99

avian flu, 23, 37

B

barriers, 82
benefits, 25, 30, 54, 90
biological, 33, 37
birds, 23, 37, 113
bonus, 42
borrowing, 11
Brownfields Program, 69
budget deficit, 98
budget resolution, vii
Bureau of Land Management (BLM), viii, 8, 9, 11, 15, 16, 17, 18, 19, 20, 77, 79, 82, 97, 99, 101, 106, 110
Bureau of Reclamation, vii, 3
Bush Administration, 36, 68, 116

C

California, 11, 16, 42, 114
canals, 102
capacity, 27, 55
capital, 35, 93, 94
certification, 90
civilian, 33
Clean Air Act, 66, 71, 72
Clean Water Act, 67
climate change, 34, 64, 66, 72
clinical, 85, 86, 88
clinics, 83, 86, 89
Clinton Administration, 100
coal, 38, 43, 44, 45, 114
coastal management, 42
coastal zone, 42
collaboration, 35
colleges, 46, 49, 50, 115
Colorado, 18
combat, 52
commercial, 18, 28, 69
commercialization, 27
Committee(s) on Appropriations, viii, 5, 7, 8, 9, 45, 105, 116
community(ies), 10, 31, 35, 66, 67, 68, 69, 80, 82, 86, 87, 94
Compact of Free Association (CFA), 55
compensation, 92
compliance, 41, 59
Compliance and Asset Management Program (CAM), 41
components, 27
Comprehensive Environmental Response, Compensation, and Liability Act (CERCLA), 68, 69
computing, 35
conditioning, 105
confidence, 92
Congress, vii, viii, 3, 4, 9, 10, 20, 23, 24, 26, 30, 36, 39, 40, 41, 51, 60, 61, 63, 64, 66, 67, 68, 70, 71, 75, 82, 91, 97, 100, 101, 102, 113, 115, 116, 117
Congressional Budget and Impoundment Control Act, vii
Congressional Record, 5, 7, 65, 113, 116, 117
conservation, 3, 17, 18, 21, 26, 27, 41
Constitution, vii
constraints, vii
construction, viii, 8, 10, 19, 31, 46, 51, 78, 83, 88, 89, 90, 92, 103, 105
Consumer Price Index, 56
contamination, 63, 68, 69
continuing, vii, 4
contracts, 46, 83, 87, 88, 93
control, 55, 63, 66, 71, 80
conversion, 28, 80
costs, 22, 30, 37, 38, 39, 40, 45, 60, 68, 75, 78, 86, 87, 89, 105, 110, 117
Council on Environmental Quality, 107
Court of Appeals, 42, 59
covering, 3, 27
crime, 52
culture, 32
curriculum, 95

D

debt, vii
decisions, 11, 42, 54, 77, 91
deduction, 38, 40
defense, 7
deficit, 98
degradation, 105
degree, 80
demand, 61
Department of Agriculture, vii, 3, 19, 75, 82
Department of Defense, 110
Department of Energy (DOE), 3
Department of Health and Human Services, vii, 3, 83
Department of Housing and Urban Development (HUD), 53
Department of Justice, 90
Department of the Interior (DOI), vii, 3, 8, 15, 18, 19, 28, 32, 41, 57, 58, 59, 60, 78, 99, 100, 101, 102, 103, 104, 106, 115
desire, 69
detection, 23, 37, 77
detention, 52, 53
diabetes, 83
disaster, 55, 86
dissatisfaction, 78
distribution, 44, 86
District of Columbia, 59
division, 93
donations, 27, 30, 95
drinking water, viii, 10, 66, 67
duties, 91, 113

E

economic, 46, 69
economic development, 46
economy, 77
ecosystem, 35, 102, 103, 105, 117
ecosystem restoration, 35
education, viii, 11, 46, 47, 48, 49, 50, 51, 54, 84, 87, 94, 95, 115, 117
Elementary and Secondary Education Act, 50
eligibility criteria, 53
elk, 28
email, 35
employees, 27, 70, 92, 93
employment, 46
endangered, 21, 22
Endangered Species Act (ESA), 21, 26
energy, 3, 15, 17, 33, 38
Energy Policy Act, 39, 65
Energy Policy Act of 2005, 39, 65
environment, 33, 69, 77
environmental, 11, 35, 45, 63, 68, 71, 77, 83, 88, 102
environmental contamination, 63
environmental protection, 45
Environmental Protection Agency (EPA), viii, 3, 4, 8, 10, 11, 63, 64, 65, 66, 67, 69, 70, 71, 72, 73, 105, 116
equipment, 52, 77, 88
estimating, 52
Everglades, 4, 102, 103, 104, 105, 111
evidence, 88
exercise, 91
expenditures, 17, 19, 59, 91, 92
experts, 54
exposure, 68
extraction, 45
eye, 43

F

failure, 91
family, 91
Far East, 37
federal budget, 98
federal funds, 27, 30, 67, 68
federal government, 33, 42, 52, 55, 59, 67, 72, 90, 105
federal law, 52, 102
Federal Register, 116

fee(s), 16, 18, 41, 43, 44, 61, 110, 114
feet, 92
fire fighting, viii, 8, 19
fire suppression, 18, 75, 77
fires, 11, 19, 77, 78
fish, 82
Fish and Wildlife Service (FWS), viii, 8, 20, 21, 23, 24, 26, 37, 97, 99, 101, 103, 104, 106, 113
fisheries, 17
fixed costs, 22, 30
Forest Service (FS), vii, viii, 3, 8, 11, 19, 20, 57, 75, 78, 79, 82, 97, 101, 102, 107, 110
Forestry, 75, 79, 80, 81
forests, 9
fuel, 11, 77, 78, 79
funding, vii, viii, 3, 4, 5, 7, 9, 10, 11, 15, 17, 18, 19, 21, 22, 24, 25, 26, 28, 29, 30, 31, 32, 33, 34, 35, 36, 38, 40, 45, 46, 50, 51, 52, 53, 55, 57, 60, 61, 63, 64, 65, 66, 67, 68, 69, 70, 71, 72, 77, 78, 79, 80, 82, 83, 85, 86, 87, 88, 89, 92, 94, 95, 97, 98, 100, 102, 103, 104, 105, 110, 113, 115, 116, 117
fundraising, 92
funds, vii, viii, 1, 3, 4, 5, 8, 9, 10, 11, 15, 17, 18, 19, 20, 21, 22, 27, 29, 30, 31, 32, 33, 36, 39, 40, 44, 45, 46, 49, 50, 51, 52, 53, 54, 55, 57, 59, 60, 65, 66, 67, 68, 69, 70, 71, 72, 75, 76, 77, 78, 79, 80, 86, 92, 93, 97, 98, 99, 100, 101, 102, 103, 105, 110, 117

G

gas, 11, 17, 18, 38, 39, 40, 41, 42
General Accounting Office
global climate change, 34
Global Warming, 34
goals, 49, 50
governance, 87, 88, 92
government, 7, 10, 11, 24, 26, 33, 35, 40, 42, 46, 52, 55, 57, 59, 63, 66, 67, 71, 72, 73, 90, 93, 97, 100, 105, 116
Government Accountability Office (GAO), 55, 115, 117
grants, 11, 21, 26, 32, 33, 43, 44, 46, 50, 55, 63, 66, 67, 69, 70, 71, 72, 88, 93, 94, 95, 99, 100
grazing, 15
groups, 27, 83
growth, 92
GSA, 104
Guam, 55
Gulf of Mexico, 40, 41, 100

H

habitat, 23, 76, 113
harvesting, 77
hazardous substances, 67
hazardous wastes, 63
hazards, 33, 36, 43
health, viii, 11, 17, 43, 51, 66, 68, 69, 80, 83, 85, 86, 87, 88, 89, 92, 110, 114
Health and Human Services (HHS), vii, 3, 83, 88, 89, 117
health care, 83, 86, 88, 89
health care costs, 86
health education, 87
health effects, 66
health information, 88
health insurance, 85
health services, 83, 85, 86, 87, 88
health status, 86
hearing, 60, 115
higher education, 46, 51
HIP, 53
homes, 90, 91
hospital(s), 83, 86, 89
House, vii, viii, 3, 4, 5, 7, 8, 9, 10, 12, 15, 16, 17, 18, 19, 20, 21, 22, 23, 24, 25, 26, 27, 28, 29, 30, 31, 32, 33, 34, 38, 39, 40, 41, 42, 45, 46, 47, 48, 49, 50, 51, 52, 53, 54, 55, 56, 58, 59, 60,

61, 63, 64, 65, 66, 68, 69, 70, 71, 72, 75, 76, 77, 78, 79, 81, 82, 83, 84, 85, 86, 87, 88, 89, 90, 91, 93, 94, 95, 98, 99, 100, 101, 102, 103, 105, 106, 107, 108, 109, 110, 114, 116, 117
House Appropriations Committee, 10, 28, 41, 50, 53, 59, 60, 76, 78, 88, 103, 110
housing, viii, 46, 53, 90
Housing and Urban Development, 4, 53, 116
human, 66, 68, 69
hunting, 28
hurricane, 22, 33
hydrological, 103

I

identity, 27
images, 35
implementation, 11, 46, 60, 72, 105
imports, 9
inclusion, 19, 32
income, 58, 93
Independent Agencies, 4, 116
Indian(s), vii, viii, 3, 8, 9, 10, 11, 15, 38, 43, 46, 47, 48, 49, 50, 52, 53, 54, 57, 58, 59, 60, 61, 83, 84, 85, 86, 87, 88, 89, 103, 104, 106, 107, 108, 110, 114, 115, 116
Indian Gaming Regulatory Act (IGRA), 61, 116
Indian Health Service (HIS), vii, viii, 3, 8, 10, 11, 83, 84, 85, 86, 87, 88, 89, 107
industrial, 69
industry, 11
inflation, 5, 57, 63, 68
information technology, 35
infrastructure, 10, 19, 35, 37, 55, 66, 67, 69, 82, 90, 91
inspections, 70
institutions, 46, 95, 115
insurance, 85
interface, 78
international, 31
invasive species, 23
investigations, 34, 35, 36
investment, 58, 92

J

jails, 52
Jefferson, 115
judge, 60
judiciary, 55
jurisdiction, 3, 30, 52, 55, 95, 116
justification, 65, 72, 90

K

Kennedy, John F., 108

L

land, viii, 3, 9, 10, 11, 15, 17, 20, 24, 32, 35, 43, 46, 57, 59, 60, 69, 76, 79, 82, 90, 97, 98, 101, 102, 113
land acquisition, viii, 10, 20, 24, 32, 76, 90, 97, 98, 101, 102, 113
Land and Water Conservation Fund (LWCF), 10, 11, 20, 24, 29, 32, 38, 97, 98, 99, 100, 101, 102, 113
land use, 43
Landsat 7, 35
language, 9, 21, 28, 39, 40, 41, 61, 72, 77, 91
law(s), 3, 4, 7, 8, 9, 15, 16, 17, 18, 19, 20, 21, 23, 25, 26, 27, 28, 29, 30, 31, 32, 33, 34, 35, 36, 37, 39, 40, 43, 44, 46, 51, 52, 53, 54, 55, 56, 63, 64, 66, 67, 68, 69, 70, 71, 72, 75, 77, 78, 80, 81, 82, 83, 85, 86, 87, 88, 89, 90, 91, 92, 93, 94, 95, 98, 99, 102, 103, 105
law enforcement, 30, 46, 52, 53, 82
lead, 23, 41, 46, 52
leadership, 92

legislation, vii, viii, 4, 28, 31, 40, 42, 56, 60, 76, 91, 92
levees, 102
Lieu of Taxes, viii, 11, 56, 57, 110
limitation, 61
litigation, 58, 59, 60, 90
livestock, 15
loans, 10, 66
local community, 31
local government, 11, 55, 57, 63, 66, 71, 97, 100
long-term, 68
LUST, 65

M

main line, 91
Maine, 23
maintenance, 17, 22, 30, 32, 37, 49, 53, 55, 75, 82, 84, 88, 89
management, ix, 8, 9, 10, 15, 16, 17, 18, 19, 23, 24, 28, 30, 35, 42, 46, 49, 57, 63, 71, 72, 75, 80, 82, 87, 88, 92, 97, 110
mapping, 33
Mariana Islands, 55
Marshall Islands, 55
matching funds, 67, 72, 103, 117
measures, vii, 86
media, 113
Medicaid, 85
medical care, 86
Medicare, 85
mental health, 86
methamphetamine, 84
Mexican, 21
Mexico, 40, 41, 100
Micronesia, 55
migratory birds, 113
mineral resources, 15, 36
minerals, 15, 17, 38, 58
Minerals Management Service (MMS), viii, 8, 11, 37, 38, 39, 40, 41, 42, 106, 110, 114
mining, 43
money, 10, 19, 31, 44, 75, 85, 88, 97, 100, 114, 115
moratorium, 40
music, 95

N

nation, 15, 33, 37, 68
National Academy of Sciences, 73
National Endowment for the Arts (NEA), 3, 94, 95, 96, 108
National Endowment for the Humanities, 3, 94, 95, 96
National Gallery, 3, 108
National Park Service (NPS), viii, 4, 8, 27, 28, 29, 30, 31, 32, 33, 97, 99, 101, 103, 104, 106
national parks, 27, 28
National Wildlife Refuge, 22, 24, 26, 97, 105
Native American, 61
natural, 3, 11, 18, 27, 31, 33, 38, 41, 46, 55, 75, 102, 103
natural gas, 11, 38, 41
natural hazards, 33
natural resources, 46
negotiating, 90
network, 36, 72
New York, 30, 40
New York Times, 40
North America, 23, 37, 101
Northeast, 23
nursing, 87

O

Office of Special Trustee (OST), viii, 9, 10, 57, 58, 59, 60, 110, 115
Office of Surface Mining (OSM), viii, 8, 43, 44, 45, 106
offshore oil, 38
oil, 11, 17, 18, 38, 39, 40, 41, 42

oil shale, 18
oil spill, 41
OMB, 50, 51, 52, 54
Oregon, 16
organizations, 46, 68, 71, 88
oversight, 35, 46, 61, 70, 92
ownership, 98

P

Pacific, 23, 40, 55
particulate matter, 72
partnership(s), 31, 95
pathogenic, 23
performance, 69, 100
permit, 18
pesticides, 63
petroleum, 3, 39
phosphorus, 105
planning, 32, 35, 37, 78, 82
polar bears, 9
police, 18, 30
pollutants, 105
pollution, 63, 66, 71, 105
population, 78
powers, 54
preference, 31
preparation, 41
preparedness, 19, 75, 77, 78
President Bush, 27
President Clinton, 98
prevention, 77, 84, 86
prices, 38
primary care, 86
priorities, 32, 72, 98
privatization, 27
procedures, 43
producers, 40
production, 11, 37, 38, 43, 44, 114
productivity, 17
professions, 88
profits, 93
program, viii, 9, 11, 17, 18, 21, 24, 25, 26, 28, 30, 31, 32, 33, 34, 35, 36, 37, 39, 40, 41, 44, 46, 49, 50, 53, 56, 57, 68, 69, 70, 77, 80, 83, 85, 87, 88, 94, 95, 97, 98, 100, 101, 114
program administration, 32, 100
property taxes, 57
public, 9, 11, 15, 17, 27, 28, 35, 40, 50, 68, 77, 87, 95, 115
public health, 87
public schools, 50

Q

questioning, 53

R

range, 17, 75
real estate, 46
reclamation, vii, viii, 3, 8, 43, 45, 106
recognition, 54
reconcile, 58
reconciliation, vii
reconstruction, 8, 78
recovery, 17, 21, 33, 114
recreation, 15, 31, 32
recreational, 17, 27, 28, 97
recreational areas, 27
reduction, 8, 11, 17, 18, 19, 20, 21, 29, 36, 44, 51, 65, 70, 77, 78, 79, 80, 82, 89, 93, 98, 110
refuge, 22, 25
regional, 83, 95
Registry, 107
regular, vii, 4, 5, 9, 23
regulation(s), 18, 28, 43, 61, 63, 66, 114
rehabilitation, 8, 18, 31, 53, 77, 78
remediation, 43, 68, 82
rent, 22, 71
repair, 31, 37, 46, 51, 82
reservation, 90
residential, 83
resolution, 4, 35

resources, 15, 17, 23, 27, 31, 33, 34, 35, 36, 37, 41, 46, 49, 52, 54, 61, 68, 71, 82, 86
restitution, 42
restructuring, 44, 116
revenue, vii, 38, 39, 40, 41, 91, 100
rings, 54
risk, 78
royalty, ix, 11, 38, 39, 40, 41, 110
rural areas, 57
rural schools, viii, 6, 8, 9, 56, 57, 76, 109, 110
Russian, 37
rust, 10, 15, 57, 60, 61, 93, 116

S

safety, 43, 51, 53, 92
salary(ies), 22, 55, 92, 93, 117
sales, 20, 77
Samoa, 55
sampling, 37, 59
sanitation, 88
satellite, 35
scholarships, 88
school, 11, 46, 49, 50, 51, 76, 83, 87, 95
science, 33, 71
scientific, 37, 41, 66, 70, 71, 72
security, 30, 35, 71, 92
seed, 10, 66
Senate, vii, viii, 3, 4, 5, 7, 8, 9, 12, 15, 16, 17, 18, 19, 20, 21, 22, 23, 24, 25, 26, 27, 28, 29, 30, 31, 32, 33, 34, 35, 38, 39, 40, 45, 46, 47, 48, 49, 50, 51, 52, 53, 54, 55, 56, 58, 60, 61, 63, 64, 65, 66, 68, 69, 70, 71, 72, 75, 78, 79, 81, 82, 83, 84, 85, 86, 87, 88, 89, 90, 91, 93, 94, 95, 98, 99, 100, 101, 102, 103, 105, 106, 107, 108, 109, 110, 115, 116
sentencing, 52
series, 9, 102
settlements, 46, 58, 116
sharing, 38, 39, 40
sign, 90
sites, 27, 28, 30, 31, 32, 43, 44, 66, 68, 69, 70, 88, 114
Smithsonian, viii, 3, 8, 91, 92, 93, 94, 108, 117
Smithsonian Institution (SI), viii, 3, 8, 91, 92, 93, 94, 108, 117
social, 46
Southeast Asia, 37
sovereignty, 54
specialists, 49
species, 21, 22, 23, 26, 113
speed, 91
SRFs, 66, 67
staffing, 23, 52, 53, 66, 70, 89
standards, 43, 66, 67, 105
State Children's Health Insurance Program (SCHIP), 85
statute of limitations, 59
statutes, vii, 55, 63
Strategic Petroleum Reserve, 3
student achievement, 46
students, 46, 50
substance abuse, 83, 86, 88
suicide, 87
Superfund, viii, 11, 64, 65, 66, 67, 68, 69, 70
supplemental, vii, 4, 5, 6, 10, 16, 18, 23, 33, 79, 110
suppression, 8, 15, 16, 18, 75, 77, 78
suspensions, 42

T

Tax Relief and Health Care Act, 43
taxes, 57
technical assistance, 27, 80, 88
technology, 35, 44
telecommunications, 35
terrorism, 98
threatened, 21, 80
threatening, 68
threshold(s), 9, 40, 41
timber, 58, 77

time, 3, 4, 9, 34, 43, 58, 63, 68, 70, 71, 98
time frame, 9
Title III, v, 4, 57, 75, 107, 109
Tongass National Forest, 9
toxic substances, 63
training, 49, 52, 77, 87
transactions, 58, 59
transportation, 49, 50
Treasury, 11, 38, 41, 43, 44, 60, 77, 85, 116
Treasury Department, 60
trend, 24, 67, 71
trial, 59
tribal, 26, 33, 35, 44, 46, 49, 50, 52, 53, 57, 58, 59, 60, 61, 83, 87, 88, 115
tribal colleges, 50, 115
tribes, 26, 43, 44, 46, 50, 52, 53, 57, 59, 60, 61, 83, 87, 89
trust, ix, 46, 57, 59, 60, 91, 93, 117
trust fund, ix, 57, 59, 60, 93, 117

U

U.S. Geological Survey, 33, 34, 37, 103, 104, 106
U.S. Treasury, 38
United States, 30, 43, 91, 114
United Tribes Technical College, 50
universities, 36, 50, 115
USDA, 101
Utah, 18

V

values, 27, 78
vegetation, 17
vehicles, 94
victims, 86
village, 83
Virginia, 23, 40
virus, 23
visual, 95
vocational, 50, 115

W

war on terror, 98
Washington, 30, 104
wastewater, viii, 10, 66, 67
water, viii, 3, 10, 23, 33, 34, 36, 37, 46, 57, 63, 66, 67, 82, 102, 103, 105
water quality, 63, 105
water quality standards, 105
water resources, 33, 34, 36, 82
water rights, 57
water supplies, 23
websites, 73, 115
wells, 18
White House, 109
wild horses, 18
wilderness, 17
wildfire(s), viii, 1, 8, 11, 15, 16, 18, 75, 77, 78
wildland, viii, 8, 11, 15, 16, 18, 19, 75, 78, 110
wildlife, 17, 26
winter, 28
writing, 105